AVRO
SHACKLETON

POSTWAR MILITARY AIRCRAFT: 3

AVRO SHACKLETON

JOHN CHARTRES

LONDON
IAN ALLAN LTD

First published 1985

ISBN 0 7110 1513 9

© John Chartres 1985

Published by Ian Allan Ltd, Shepperton, Surrey;
and printed by Ian Allan Printing Ltd at their works
at Coombelands in Runnymede, England

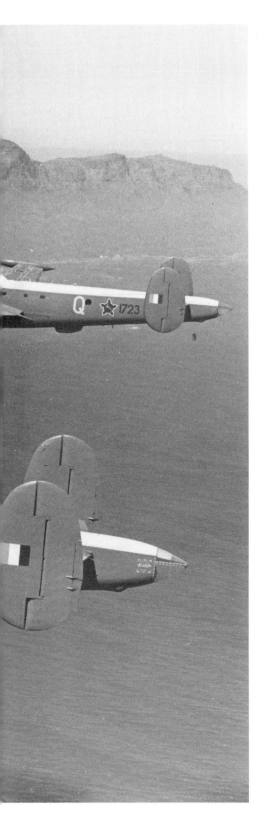

Contents

Cover:
AEW2. *Peter R. March*

Acknowledgements

It is always difficult for a 'lay' author like myself to know where to begin and end this small but important part of a semi-technical book.

On this occasion I would like to begin by thanking the scores of 'old Shackleton hands', ranging in previous rank from Aircraftman to Group Captain, who responded to my appeals for information published in *RAF News* and *Air Mail*, the newsletter of the Royal Air Forces Association. Their contributions ranged from long and thoughtful letters, through the loans of precious photographs, to the despatch of some highly revealing tape cassettes. Many enjoyable personal meetings ensued. Some, but not all, are mentioned by name in the text and in picture captions.

My thanks go again to the staff of the Air Historical Branch (RAF), especially to Grp Capt T.C. Flanagan MSc, BA (Hons), RAF (Retd), a former Shackleton navigator and Nimrod squadron commander.

They go also to many former A.V. Roe personnel, some still working under the British Aerospace umbrella, particularly Mr Harry Holmes and Mr J.H. ('Jimmy') Orrell. Although many of the pictures are credited to British Aerospace as the suppliers I believe a substantial proportion of them are the work of that great aviation photographer, Mr Paul Cullerne. For many details of the first beginnings I am indebted to the late Mr Roy Chadwick's daughter, Mrs Margaret Dove.

Mr Peter J. Howard's *Aircraft Profile No 243* was of immense help in checking details and I am indebted to his publisher for permission to extract information from it.

I could not have begun without benefit of the encyclopaedic knowledge of Manchester air historian Mr Brian Robinson, and Mr Louis Vosloo supplied me with most of the factual information and all the photographs relating to the South African Air Force Shackletons.

Among the many friends I made (and like to think I will keep) in No 8 Squadron RAF I must especially thank Wg Cdr David Greenway and his successor as CO, Wg Cdr Malcolm Cooper; Flt Lt Andy Thomas, Master Engineer Ray Donovan and Corp Chris Twiner of the Lossiemouth Station Photographic Section.

In the course of the research these and others have referred to the Shackleton variously as 'The White Monster', 'The Old Grey Lady', '10,000 rivets flying in close formation', 'the contra-rotating Nissen hut' and 'The Lovely Old Beast'. I prefer the last nickname and count myself privileged to be one of 'the last of the many' to have flown in an operational, four-piston-prop, tail-wheeled 'heavy' of the RAF in the mid-1980s.

John Chartres
Hale
Cheshire

Below:
AEW Mark 2 No WL741 of No 8 Squadron on patrol. *MoD.*

Introduction

Air Ministry Specification R5/46, issued on 17 March 1947, led to the creation of the Avro Type 696 – the aircraft which was soon to gain the immortal name of Shackleton. This specification could have its origins traced back to the very first appreciations of the value of the flying machine to admirals and generals at the turn of this century.

To naval and military minds aircraft fall into three main categories. There are those which can see over the horizon (reconnaissance aircraft), those which can deliver weapons at longer range than guns or other devices (bombers) and those which can defeat enemies bent on similar tasks (fighters). Some military aeroplanes fall into other categories: those which can carry troops into battle, those which can rescue wounded troops and others in distress, those which can carry out such mundane tasks as delivering stores, people and mail to the right places, and those which can be used to teach others to fly them. The Avro Type 696 has performed all those tasks except one: it was never a fighter even though its last user, No 8 Squadron RAF, still proudly paints fighter squadron markings on its aircraft.

At the early beginnings of naval and military aviation the mariners quite logically opted for a form of aeroplane which could take off from, and alight on, the sea as their best means of looking over the horizon and beyond from a point higher than that of the topmast of a man-of-war.

In July 1908 the post of Naval Air Assistant was proposed at the Admiralty. In September 1911 No 1 Royal Naval Airship, ironically christened 'Mayfly', crashed and was wrecked soon after take-off. On 18 November 1911 the first ascent from water by a British seaplane was achieved by Cdr Oliver Schwann in an Avro biplane from Barrow-in-Furness. On 10 January 1912 the first take-off from the deck of a British warship was achieved by Lt C.R. Sampson in a Short S-27 from the foredeck of HMS *Africa* in Sheerness harbour. On 9 May 1912 the first British flight from a

Above:
AEW Mk 2 No WR963 of No 8 Squadron on patrol. *MoD*

ship under way was achieved by Lt R. Gregory RN in a Short-27 from HMS *Hibernia* in Weymouth Bay. On 13 May 1912 a Royal Flying Corps was formed with naval and military Wings. On 1 July 1914 the Royal Naval Air Service was created as a separate entity and shortly after went to war in France, as did the by then essentially 'military' Royal Flying Corps.

Those dates and facts may not at first sight appear to have much relevance to the evolution of the Shackleton aircraft in 1949 and its continued service at least until 1985, but they relate to the establishment of principles upon which the designs of all subsequent 'maritime' aircraft have been based.

The 'ownership' of the nation's maritime combat aircraft has often varied between the Royal Navy and of the Royal Air Force since the latter Service's creation on 1 April 1918. There have been frequent disputes, and to some extent the arguments continue.

Below:
An early side-view sketch of the Mk 1 Shackleton.

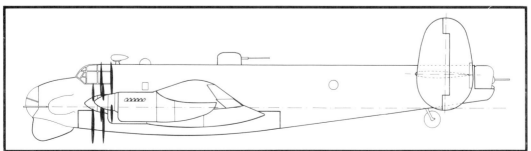

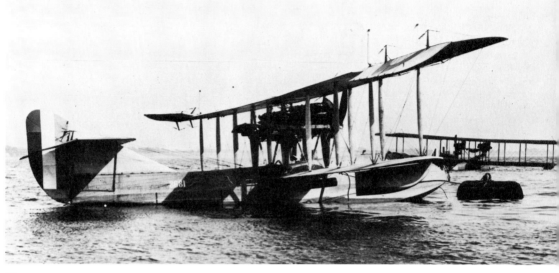

Above:
A maritime reconnaissance/anti-submarine aircraft of World War 1 – the Curtiss H-12 'Large America'.   *MoD*

In the aviation literature of World War 1 the achievements of the Royal Naval Air Service flying boat squadrons went almost unnoticed compared with the space and wordage given to those of the fighter squadrons on the Western Front ('Biggles' and the rest); yet they may have altered the course of that colossal conflict substantially with their Curtis and Porte aircraft which not only frightened many German U-boats away from their nefarious tasks but which sank a great many of them as well.

Between the wars many complicated political and inter-Service battles took place over whether the Royal Navy or the relatively new Royal Air Force should have control over the naval air arm to police the seas which the British nation still dominated – even by then quite a large share of the world's oceans. The Navy had by then acquired a reasonable fleet of aircraft carriers, and the Fleet Air Arm was created to provide the aircrews and maintainers to fly and look after what were relatively new additions to the armament of warships.

In the 1930s the phrase 'Fleet Air Arm' meant 'The Fleet Air Arm of the Royal Air Force', and many photographs are extant of a mixture of sailors in square rig and RAF personnel in pale blue forage caps equally bent on securing the safety of such aeroplanes as Fairey Flycatchers and Seals, which were flying off and on to the decks of carriers like HMS *Courageous* in the Mediterranean and thereabouts. The pilots of those days could equally be Sub-Lieutenants (A) of the Royal Navy (regarded as a rather low form of human life by their admirals), or Pilot and Flying Oficers of

the RAF. The crews in the two and three-seater aircraft were often at most rated as Leading Seamen, but frequently proudly bore the badge of 'TAG', meaning Telegraphist Air Gunner.

While the Royal Navy pursued its policy of using carrier-based aircraft to 'look-over-the-horizon-and-beyond', the Royal Air Force concentrated upon the flying boat as its mean of obtaining the long distance information which its own air marshals, and possibly admirals and generals from the other Services, would require in the next war.

The Royal Air Force at that period had settled on the flying boat as the best form of aircraft design to enable it to carry out the multiplicity of tasks which the nation then required of it – colonial policing at very long range and on a world-wide basis, 'showing the flag', and perhaps most importantly the still little-known art of anti-submarine warfare.

Thus were created the maritime squadrons of the The Royal Air Force, many but not all bearing '200-plus' numbers indicating that they had their origins in the very first squadrons of the Royal Naval Air Service – the present No 201 Squadron RAF, flying Mk 2 Nimrods from Kinloss takes its history from No 1 Squadron RNAS, and *could* claim to be the senior organisation of the whole of the The Royal Air Force (but doesn't really argue often with No 1 Squadron RAF, which takes its history from the Royal Flying Corps).

The maritime squadrons at one stage called themselves the 'Flying Boat Union' with their own small tradition of leaving their brass tunic buttons unpolished so that they took on a special verdigris hue.

The flying boat squadrons first made their names with one of the first post-World War 1 large aircraft designs, the Supermarine Southampton. Nos 201, 203,

204, 205 and 210 Squadrons flew these boats with their 15,200lb loaded weights, 83mph cruising speeds and maximum 930-mile range to most corners of the then British Empire. These and other squadrons in the 'Flying Boat Union' later moved on to bigger and better aircraft such as the Blackburn Iris and Perth, the Short Stranraer, the Saro London and finally the immortal Sunderland.

The 'Union' proved between the wars that the Royal Air Force could operate and make its presence felt on world-wide basis at relatively low cost, since it had no requirements for expensive land bases and large airfields. However, although smallish bombs could be, and were, carried on the biplane flying boats, and machine guns were mounted, not all that much emphasis was placed in the training schedules on the black art of anti-submarine warfare which was to dominate the employment of maritime aircraft for the next half-century. At least not until the Sunderlands arrived.

At a fairly early stage in the RAF's expansion Coastal Command was created on 14 July 1936. Its first commanders, Air Marshals Sir Arthur Longmore and Philip Joubert de la Ferte, saw the need for a combination of flying boats and land-based aircraft to meet their designated tasks, and by the outbreak of World War 2 the Command 'owned' not only a mix of Sunderlands and various types of biplane boats but two squadrons of Ansons (Nos 48 and 206). It also rapidly acquired a sort of 'maritime Dad's Air Force' of Tiger and Hornet Moths organised into Coastal Patrol Flights, their aircrews' survival equipment consisting of one signal pistol, a car tyre inner tube and two pigeons. Coastal Command went to war with 450 aircraft and emerged at the end of it with more than a

Below:
One of the last flying Sunderlands, in French markings, being escorted in to Britain by Mk 3 Shackletons of No 201 Squadron before taking up 'permanent residence' at the RAF Museum, Hendon. *MoD*

Bottom:
A Coastal Command Hudson fitted with airborne lifeboat. *MoD*

million flying hours on record, a high proportion of them logged in Sunderlands.

This aircraft type justifiably earned a place in the affections of the British public and the question is often asked: 'Why was the flying boat abandoned in the general development of long range maritime aircraft?' It is a valid question. Part of the answer lies in the fallacy that a flying boat can alight and take off from any sort of water and in any sort of weather. Large flying boats like Sunderlands look to be capable of coping with anything that Nature can throw at them in the air or on the water, but in fact they are fragile indeed when attempting to alight on rough open seas and have even more difficulty taking off again. Because of the essential configuration of a flying boat hull it is also aerodynamically inefficient, meaning that more power and therefore more fuel has to be employed to achieve the desirables of speed and range than for equivalent sized land-planes. Towards the middle of World War 2, with the Battle of the Atlantic becoming a critical (if not *the* critical) factor, the land-based maritime aircraft was already begining to win favour.

By then, apart from its Sunderland and Catalina boats, Coastal Command was operating many medium range land planes such as Hudsons, Venturas and Wellingtons and began to add to its fleet a formidable force of VLR (Very Long Range) Liberators, Fortresses and Halifaxes adapted to the maritime role and capable of reaching further across the Atlantic.

By this period too the role of Coastal Command aircraft had moved on from that of pure reconnaissance, especially the spotting of enemy surface shipping, into the combined one of their also being 'hunter-killers' of submarines. The Sunderlands and Catalinas and some other type often performed this latter role valiantly, albeit with only rudimentary

'hunting' equipment strongly dependent on the human eyeball Mk 1, and their kills tended to be sufficiently rare to be occasions for great rejoicing.

History later proved that perhaps their greatest effectiveness lay in the sheer deterrent of their presence overhead, forcing U-boats to stay submerged. The argument has been advanced in recent years that the diversion of more four-engined heavies from the area bombing of Germany to the Atlantic might have shortened the war. The tallies show that nearly 300 German U-boats were sunk by aircraft alone, many more by combinations of ships and aircraft.

As the Battle of the Atlantic raged on another requirement emerged; that of long-range air-sea rescue.

The Command's first land-based VLRs were Liberator Mk 1s issued to No 120 Squadron at Nutt's Corner in Northern Ireland in 1941. They had an operational range of 2,400 miles compared with the Sunderlands' 1,300, and a maximum speed of 270mph compared with the latter's seldom attained 213mph. They were followed by Mk 3s built under contract in Britain and 3As supplied under Lend-Lease, the type eventually equipping 12 Coastal Command squadrons. Although the majority of these highly effective aircraft had to be returned to the States soon after the war some GR (General Reconnaissance) Mk 8s remained in the Command until 1947.

Boeing B-17 Fortress Mks 1, 2 and 3 served in Nos 59, 206 and 220 Squadrons of Coastal Command as well as in Nos 251, 517, 519 and 521 (Met) Squadrons. The RAF Fortress 1s which had survived somewhat disastrous European bombing raids were first based with Coastal Command at Benbecula, Scotland in October 1942 and were replaced with Fortress 2s a year later.

The end of hostilities by no means meant the end of Coastal Command's responsibilities in the far Atlantic. The creation of NATO was imminent and the

Below:
Coastal Command Liberators. *Imperial War Museum*

Above:
AN ASR 3 Lancaster with airborne lifeboat.

Right:
Lifeboat being fitted to ASR 3 Lancaster. *IWM*

Below right:
The RAF's last MR3 Lancaster, RF325, going out of service at St Eval in October 1956.

requirement for long range air-sea rescue aircraft remained as great as ever. As a temporary expedient the Command turned to the Lancaster to replace its American VLRs.

The first maritime Lancasters, designated ASR (Air-Sea Rescue) Mk 3s, were Cunliffe-Owen Ltd – conversions of Mk 3 bombers, and some were fitted with the airborne lifeboats designed by the yachtsman extraordinary Uffa Fox. They were followed by GR (General Reconnaissance) 3s. The ASR, GR and MR Lancasters equipped four UK-based Coastal squadrons as well as Nos 37 and 38 Squadrons based in Malta. (The RAF's very last Lancaster, MR3 No RF325, was finally retired from service with the School of Maritime Reconnaissance at St Mawgan, Cornwall, on 15 October 1956.)

By the mid-1940s the need for a better VLR aircraft for Coastal Command was paramount, particularly in terms of crew comfort, or at least crew survival in terms of them being able to do their jobs efficiently on missions which could last 18 hours or more. That constituted the essence of the operational requirement issued in March 1946 and met by Avro Type 696. Very little commercial competition was involved in the aircraft industry: the first contract for three prototypes and 29 production aircraft inevitably went to A.V. Roe Ltd of Manchester.

1
The Creation of 'Type 696'

By the time that Specification R5/46 dropped through letterboxes in Manchester, Avro Lincolns, the 'stretched' Lancasters primarily produced for a conventional war against the Japanese mainland, had been in RAF service for more than a year. A Mk 3 maritime version of the Lincoln had been under consideration but Coastal Command wanted a fundamental improvement for its postwar tasks – something much bigger and better, and most importantly providing more comfort for crews it knew were going to have to take on exceptionally demanding tasks over the great oceans which Britain and her Allies still had to dominate. (The description 'Lincoln 3' was loosely used for 'Type 696' for a time but meant something very different from the first concept.)

Mr Roy Chadwick CBE, MSc, ERSA, FRAeS, AMCT, possessor of the master mind behind the Lancaster and of so many successful aeroplanes before it, was still in the design 'chair' at A.V. Roe, though he was shortly to be promoted from Chief Designer to Technical Director. While much of the detailed work on Type 696 was carried out by others, it was his concept. As usual he personally supervised everything that was happening 'on the boards' and it was he who gave it the name of Shackleton. His choice lay partly in the fact that it was an entirely appropriate one for an aircraft which was going to voyage over vast distances

Below:
The Avro Lincoln. *British Aerospace*

Right:
Mr Roy Chadwick, the tall figure on right, talking to the Queen at Woodford in November 1942. *Manchester Evening News*

Below right:
Artist's impression of the Shackleton GR Mk 1. *British Aerospace*

but he also picked the name because his wife Mary was descended from the great explorer's family. Furthermore, he had designed the little Avro Antarctic seaplane for Sir Ernest Shackleton's last expedition in 1921. Roy Chadwick's daughter, Mrs Margaret Dove, has clear memories of her father coming home with early sketches and telling the family of the choice of name.

He was not of course to see this, the last of his 'heavies', bearing the unmistakable stamp of a designer who believes that 'it should *look* right', make its first flight.

On Saturday 24 August 1947 he boarded the Tudor II prototype G-AGSU for what should have been a routine test flight from Woodford to check out some minor vibration problems and evaluate some new research instruments. Mr S.A. ('Bill') Thorn, the company's Chief Test Pilot, was at the controls and

Above:
An early example of the ill-fated Avro Manchester from which the Shackleton 'shape' finally evolved. Mr Chadwick himself was never happy about this design because financial stringencies in the 1930s had restricted him to the employment of only two Rolls-Royce Vulture engines. Once he had, on his own initiative, up-powered the airframe to four Rolls-Royce Merlins and re-named it 'Lancaster' it was an immediate success as the world knows. *British Aerospace*

Below:
Close-ups of the 'translation' unit required for a contra-rotating propeller assembly. *both British Aerospace*

Right:
A Spitfire F.21 (LA215) of the Central Fighter Establishment with Griffon and contra-rotating propellors. *MoD*

there were four others on board, including Mr Stuart Davies who had succeeded Chadwick as Chief Designer.

Above left:
**The advanced Martin-Baker F18/39 fighter of January 1945
which did not go into production. It was powered by a
Griffon with contra-rotating propellors and was probably the
first aircraft to fly with this propulsion arrangement. Mr
'Jimmy' Martin of Martin-Baker played a large part in the
evolution of the necessarily complicated gearing
arrangement.**

Left:
**A Griffon-powered Mk XIV Spitfire of the Indian Air Force
circa 1945/46 near Peshawar.**
Norman Edwards Associates (Manchester)

Above:
**The comforting view from the co-pilot's window of a
Shackleton.** *Rolls-Royce*

As later inquiries substantiated there had been a
tragic error in the rigging of the aileron controls (they
were reversed) and the aircraft crashed from 50ft into a
pond on the edge of the airfield, killing Chadwick and
three others – Bill Thorn, Sqn Ldr David Wilson, chief
of the Flight Test Section, and Mr Joseph Webster, the
radio operator. Mr Davies, who had been positioned
towards the rear of the aircraft escaped with minor
injuries – he later master-minded the design of the
Vulcan bomber – and the flight engineer, Mr Talbot,
survived with severe multiple injuries. It was a disaster
for the whole nation.

Those who worked on the detailed design of Type
696 recall it as one of the more straightforward tasks
undertaken at the Avro Chadderton and Woodford
factories, and certainly a low-cost one. 'All we really
did "on the boards" was to slit the Lancaster and
Lincoln fuselage shape from end to end and make it
about two-foot fatter all round', recalls Mr Don

Andrew, project designer at the time. That is perhaps
an over-simplification but certainly Lincoln wing and
Tudor undercarriage components were incorporated,
and the overall shape of the Manchester-Lancaster-
Lincoln lineage was retained.

There was of course one other fundamental change –
the adoption of Rolls-Royce Griffon engine with
contra-rotating airscrews, powerplants which had
been developed first to meet requirements for later
generations of Fleet Air Arm and RAF fighters.
Griffons had already proved themselves in the last
Marks of Seafire, Firefly and Barracuda, and the
contra-rotating screw arrangement went into a
revolutionary Martin-Baker fighter design (which did
not see production) and was adopted for service in
some very late Marks of Spitfires.

The first brochure issued by A.V. Roe & Co Ltd on
the 'Avro Type 696 Maritime Reconnaissance
Aircraft' on 29 January 1946 read:

'The AVRO TYPE NO. 696 is a four-engined mid-
wing monoplane developed from the AVRO
LINCOLN and the AVRO TUDOR to perform the
duties of a MARITIME RECONNAISSANCE
AIRCRAFT.

'The AVRO TYPE NO. 696, therefore consists of
TUDOR outer wings and undercarriage, a modified
LINCOLN centre section, a wider and deeper
fuselage, and finally a LINCOLN tail unit.

'The wider and deeper fuselage will provide
adequate headroom and walkway space for the crew.
Rest positions and a small galley for the crew are
provided and the fuselage is soundproofed from the
cockpit to the crew's rest position. Adequate heating

will be provided for the crew stations, including the mid-upper and rear turrets.

'This aircraft will mount heavier nose armament than the LINCOLN, it being proposed to carry two 20mm cannons, one on each side of the nose in a barbette.

'Both front gunner and bomb aimer can be accommodated in the nose of the aircraft, and this nose, largely transparent, provides a good search position which is supplemented by two beam lookouts aft. Mid-upper and rear turrets are as on the LINCOLN.

'Provision is made for carrying a 12,000lb bomb within the bomb doors, or several "dealers", or a mixed load. The bomb floor is continued aft on the same level, as a walkway for the crew to the lookout stations and galley, the head room remaining the same.

'Provision has also been made for Air Sea rescue work, carrying a lifeboat with two beam lookout

stations for the crew aft. Provision is also made for the carriage of flares.'

In the event the final design was not quite as straightforward as all that. The tailplane, fin and rudder arrangements and shapes on Type 696 varied from those of the Lincoln, although not all that obviously. In some respects the 'crew comfort' descriptions in the brochure turned out to be somewhat euphoric.

Preliminary performance figures given in this brochure were based on the use of Rolls-Royce Merlin 85 engines with the suggestion that Griffons could be fitted as alternatives. The preliminary figures indicated a maximum speed of 300mph at 18,300ft, a service ceiling of 25,700 and an absolute ceiling of 27,000, a maximum range of 3,800 miles (at an average speed of 200mph) and a gross weight of 82,000lb. They were formidable figures for the decade but modest ones in terms of the ultimate development of the type.

The Mk 1 prototype Shackleton, WV126, first flown by Avro's Chief Test Pilot Mr J. H. ('Jimmy') Orrell from Woodford on 9 March 1949, was powered by four 2,450hp Griffon 57 engines driving six-bladed contra-rotating screws evolved by de Havilland Propellors Ltd (now part of British Aerospace) of Lostock near Bolton. The desirable but complicated airscrew design had involved co-operation with Rolls-Royce and some special help from Mr 'Jimmy' Martin of Martin-Bakers who solved the particular problem of lubricating the heat-and-friction producing point at the hub end with his 'wrap-around' translation unit. Shackleton captains and flight engineers to this day go through a little routine of easing back revolutions on each engine every few hours to enable oil to be sucked into this translation unit under the principle worked out by a remarkable engineer (who among other things designed a stainless steel plate to replace his own cranium which had been badly fractured by maurauders who attacked him in his home).

The Griffon engine was originally developed to meet Fleet Air Arm requirements for high power at low altitude. The Griffon, with a bore of 6.0 and a stroke of 6.6, was 27% greater in capacity than the most advanced Merlin yet was only 3in longer and 0.4sq ft greater in frontal area. More than 6,000 Griffons were built during World War 2 – they were the last in the line of the great Rolls-Royce V-12s, spanning 40 years and beginning with the 'R' engine in the S-6s which won the Schneider Trophy outright in 1931 and gave birth to the Spitfire. One of the phrases still heard at the time of writing this book is that the

Left:
'Jimmy' Orrell, circa 1950. *British Aerospace*

Right:
'Jimmy' Orrell runs up preparatory to the first take-off on 9 march 1949 . . . and is airborne after 14 seconds.
both British Aerospace

Above left:
A 'Farnborough spectacular'. *British Aerospace*

Left:
The first prototype, VW126. *British Aerospace*

Above:
Mk 2 prototype WB833. This aircraft was eventually lost in a crash in April 1968 while in RAF service. *British Aerospace*

'Griffon Growl' will still be heard over the shores and waters of Britain until the last Shackleton is taken out of service, which again on news at the time of writing may be after the appearance of this book on the shelves. To this writer the 'Griffon Growl' is much akin to that of a Merlin in the skies, which to those battling on the ground meant 'It's one of ours'. It is a sound which will conjure up much emotion until all the air, land and sea warriors of World War 2 have moved on to hopefully higher altitudes.

The first engine installation trials for the Type 696 were carried out at the Rolls-Royce Hucknall aerodrome in Derbyshire, with two modified Lancastrian IIs – the Lancastrian was Avro's first attempt to make a civil airliner out of the Lancaster, and was followed by the not very successful Tudor, referred to above. The Lancastrians were fitted with Griffon inboard engines and Merlin outers.

At about the same time, Mr J.D. ('Johnny') Baker of Avro's test pilot staff was seeking the views of Coastal Command crews as to what they wanted from a new GR (General Reconnoissance) or MR (Maritime Reconnaissance) aircraft. He particularly sought the views of the crews of the Lancaster GR3s operating from Malta. Their views were fairly clear cut – more room, less noise and the opportunity to consume hot drink and food on flights lasting longer than the average civilian's two working days.

The recollections of Jimmy Orrell, now into his 82nd year, of the first flight of VW126 on 9 March 1949 are still crystal clear. Like any other test pilot (and Jimmy had tested no fewer than *900* different Lancasters from Woodford) he did some cautious taxy tests. He was not entirely happy about the amount of 'boot' he needed on the rudders and took VW126 back for the addition of some tape-and-glue trimmers.

He then lfited off after a 14-second run, with Mr S.E. Esler as co-pilot and Mr A. Blake as flight engineer, and flew '126' round Woodford for 33 minutes. After a little more 'trimming and straking' with fabric and glue on the tail he later made another 45-minute flight. To this day he cannot remember any particular problems and is apt to wonder what he would have thought at the time if he had known that this aeroplane was to go on flying operationally for close on 40 years.

'Like all of Roy Chadwick's Avro designs it just felt right and I never had any worries' said a pilot who had graduated on Avro 504s, flown Sopwith Snipes in peacetime, done his share of joy-riding from beaches, flown HP42s for Imperial Airways and gone on flying civil-registered airliners such as Ensigns and Albatrosses in war conditions until he joined Avros in 1942. 'I think we all knew it was going to be a good aircraft from the start. After all it had the "Chadwick Stamp" on it.'

VW126 was something of a one-off aircraft, being fitted with the twin 20mm guns in a nose barbette, a tail turret designed to take two 0.5 guns and a flight refuelling point under the tail – three features which did not appear even in the second and third prototypes, VW131 and VW135. The barbette nose gun arrangement was found to be inefficient, the tail gun turret caused centre of gravity problems, and the flight refuelling point was considered 'superfluous to requirements'. The basic dimensions however remained as a span of 120ft (similar to that of the Lincoln), overall length of 87ft 3in (9ft more than that of the Lincoln) and a loaded weight of 86,000lb. In addition to the later modified nose and tail gun positions the design incorporated a dorsal Bristol B-17 turret to house twin 20mm cannons for self-defence.

The bomb bay was designed to carry up to 20,000lb of weapons or maritime stores such as flares and rescue dinghies, or a mix of each.

Accommodation was for a 10-man crew consisting of two pilots, two navigators, a flight engineer and five crewmen with various signalling, gunnery and general tasks, including cooking. The crew comfort aspect took high priority with that feature of 'standing headroom throughout' – still used in yacht manufacturers' brochures – emphasised in A.V. Roe's sales literature.

It was, however, accepted from the start that the Mk 1 Shackleton was something of a rush job, largely because the RAF's need for something better than the Lancaster GR3 was pressing. Work on the development of the Mk 2 Shackleton began even before the first production Mk 1s went into RAF service.

The first prototype, VW126, was in fact rebuilt during the winter of 1950/51 as an 'aerodynamic' prototype of the Mk 2 and flew in this form in July 1951, with the lengthened nose and tail configuration to be seen to this day in the Airborne Early Warning

Shackletons still in operational service with No 8 Squadron RAF from Lossiemouth.

Apart from some special taxying and ground-handling problems one of the first defects discovered in the Mk 1 layout was the positioning of the radar scanner housing in the nose: second prototype VW131 had its radome smashed in a bird strike on return from early tropical trials at Khartoum in 1950. A 360° scan for the radar was obviously also desirable and a decision was made to place it in a retractable 'dustbin' below and to the aft end of the fuselage – a device reminiscent of the gun position in the RAF's last biplane bomber, the Handley Page Heyford of the 1930s.

One other early design change involved the fitting of the slightly more powerful Griffon 57A engines all round instead of 57s in the outboard positions, and the designation Mk 1A was adopted – all the original Mk 1s being brought up to this standard very quickly indeed.

Nevertheless, the first 29 production Mk 1s were delivered to the RAF during 1950/51, the first operational aircraft going in March 1951 to No 120 Squadron then based at Kinloss, Morayshire, alongside the embryo No 236 Operational Conversion Unit. Three aircraft went to the Air Sea Warfare Development Unit at St Mawgan in Cornwall for weapon development and installation trials. The OCU at Kinloss received its first Shackletons in May 1951 and No 224 Squadron in Gibraltar converted to them from its Handley Page Halifax Met Mk 6s between July and October of the same year.

Other squadrons to receive the aircraft in the mid-1950s were No 220 (re-formed at Kinloss in September 1951 and then moving to St Eval, Cornwall); No 269 (re-formed at Gibraltar and moved to Ballykelly, Northern Ireland); No 240 (re-formed at St Eval and moved to Ballykelly); and No 42 (re-formed at St Eval). By 1952 the deployment of Coastal Command squadrons was mainly dictated by the requirements of NATO, formally established three years earlier; and the Shackletons plus the remaining Sunderlands were given the long range tasks, with the airfields in the North of Scotland, Northern Ireland and West Cornwall obvious jumping-off places for the Atlantic. Northern coastal waters were covered by Lockheed Neptune and some other middle-range aircraft, most of them based at Topcliffe in Yorkshire.

With the NATO task in hand aircrews at first

Above right:
Another 'Farnborough spectacular' with the first prototype. Note the bomb doors open and both port engines feathered. *British Aerospace*

Right:
A Coastal Command Neptune. *MoD*

greeted the Mk 1 Shackletons with delight. Former Sergeant Signaller Alister ('Dinty') More AFC remembers that the Shackleton with its large crew requirement engendered 'a great spirit'. He recalls that in the early 1950s many of the aircrew had had long experience in four-engined heavy bombers and a fairly high proportion had been made prisoners-of-war, leaving them with a slightly irreverent view of authority. He says that they all looked upon 'The Great White Monster' as something of a revelation.

'Dinty' More's recollections (delivered to the author in the form of a half-hour tape cassette) go on:

'It had a rest bed, a galley, new radar and sonics and you could actually walk around in it.

'It had a number of drawbacks, It was very *very* noisy, and another problem was the heaters. They were American made and when it was cold they didn't work; they smelt, and it was not unknown for them to blow back.

'But it was great to be able to get a hot meal aboard even if they weren't all up to cordon bleu standards.'

After 10 years as an NCO aircrewman on Shackletons, Dinty More left the Service temporarily but returned to become a helicopter rescue winchman (winning his AFC as a Master Air Electronics Operator for his part in the collier *Amberley* rescue of 1973) and he says:

'I look back on the Shackleton with great affection. The Shacks were great fun to be in. The Shack didn't quite have the "aura" of a Lanc but it was much more comfortable than a Lincoln.

'It was noisy, it vibrated, it was draughty, it threw exhaust stubs, its heaters didn't work properly but in its day it was the best anti-submarine aircraft in the world.'

Former Sergeant Navigator Gordon Marsden has recalled to me some recent flights to Malta in modern jets. 'Not so noisy as the Shack and a bit faster, but NO CHARACTER', he says.

The rest of this book will be about an aeroplane which certainly has 'character'.

2
Development of the Marks and Phases

The first prototype began manufacturer's trials at Boscome Down Aeroplane & Armament Experimental Establishment in April 1949. The second prototype (VW131) first appeared in almost exactly the same configuration at the 1949 SBAC Farnborough display, flown by Mr Johnny Baker – guns were fitted in the turrets and the tail-end flight refuelling point was blanked over. During the official trials at Boscombe the nose cannon barbettes and tail turret were removed from VW131 which went on to carry out the tropical trails from Khartoum. The third prototype (VW135) first flew in March 1950, again without the nose barbette, tail turret and flight refuelling point and was mainly used for armament development trials at Boscombe.

The first production aircraft, VP254, actually flew

Below:
Yet another 'Farnborough spectacular', possibly a return after having left the arena the day before and stayed airborne until this touch-down picture was taken. *British Aerospace*

the day before the third prototype, and VP255 was seen at the Farnborough RAF display in 1950 as a static exhibit. The next to fly, VP257, was demonstrated at the Farnborough SBAC display in September of that year again by Johnny Baker. (Shackleton 'spectaculars' became a popular part of the SBAC displays for several years among the more impressive demonstrations being fly-pasts on steadily decreasing engines and take-offs one day with a return on the next after 20 hours or so airborne.)

Forty-seven Mk 1As were built in addition to the 29 production Mk 1s. The Mk 1 serials were VP254–VP268 and VP281–VP294; Mark 1A serials were WB818–WB832, WB834–WB837, WB844–WB861, WG507–WG511 and WG525–WG529.

Mk 1s and 1As were issued to Nos 32, 120, 203, 204, 205, 206, 210, 220, 224, 240 and 269 Squadrons. Other went to the Air Sea Warfare Development Unit, No 236 OCU (later MOTU – Maritime Operational Training Unit) and the Joint Anti-Submarine School Flight.

Above left:
Shackleton Mk 1 VP256 in its natural element. The Coastal Command colour scheme of the time was apt to be spoiled by the output of the Griffon exhausts. *British Aerospace*

Left:
A T-4 of MOTU photographed in 1965. *John Latimer*

Above:
A Mk 1 on final approach somewhere!

In 1956 a decision was made to concentrate Coastal Command aircrew training at Kinloss in the unit styled MOTU instead of it being split between the School of Maritime Reconnaissance (flying Lancaster GR3s) at St Mawgan and No 236 (Shackleton) OCU at Kinloss. A contributory reason was that at this period the medium range Neptunes were being phased out and the Shackleton recognised as the standard Coastal Command aircraft for many years to come. Seventeen Mk 1As were converted into T4 trainers, carrying additional radar positions, this alteration beng facilitated by the removal of the mid-upper turrets. (The T-4s were later replaced by 10 training versions of the Mk 2 and slightly confusingly called 'T-2s'.

The total of 76 Mk 1 and 1A aircraft flew at first in the then standard Coastal Command colour scheme of medium sea grey upper surfaces, white under surfaces and fuselage sides. Squadron serial letters were painted on the nose and individual aircraft letters towards the tail, this arrangement being reversed between 1956 and 1959. This colour scheme was changed to dark sea grey overall in 1955 but with white fuselage tops and full squadron numbers later painted on the rear fuselage sides.

As already stated the first prototype VW126 went back into the Avro factories at an early stage to re-emerge in mid-1951 as an 'aerodynamic' prototype of the Mk 2, with lengthened nose and tail cone (the former containing upper and lower transparent lookout positions), twin retractable tail wheels and a dummy retractable radome position on the fuselage bottom just aft of the wing. Because of the urgent need to rectify the shortcomings of the Mk 1 layout a Mk 1A (WB833) was taken off the production line and built to Mk 2 standards as the first full prototype. The braking system on the Mk 1 design had also given rise to a number of taxying problems, particularly in crosswinds, and the Mk 2s included an important improvement in the form of toe brakes and lockable rudders. The Mk 2's nose incorporated a Boulton Paul 'N' turret with two 20mm Hispano cannons remotely controlled from the upper lookout position and a bomb-aimer's position in the lower transparent portion. The tail cone was also made transparent, primarily to enable visual assessments to be made ot attacks by bomb or depth charge – this and the prone bomb aimer's position in the nose were later to prove invaluable in the search and rescue role.

Both the Mk 2 and the later Mk 3 Shackletons also bore 'Phase' designations, most of these relating to changes in electronic equipment and weapons, but sometimes to more drastic changes clearly visible from the exterior.

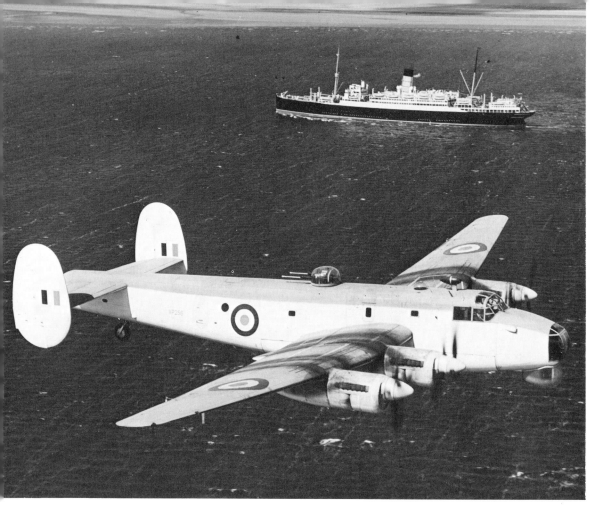

The Mk 2's maximum weight went up to 95,000lb in the Phase 3 version, demanding a lot even from Griffon 58s with water methanol boost systems.

The first production Mk 2 went to Boscombe Down in September 1952; WG533 went to RAF Manby a month later mainly for pilots' notes compilation; and WG532 went to the Anti-Submarine Warfare Development Unit in January 1953.

Seventy Maritime Reconnaissance Mk 2s were built: they carried serials WB833; WG530–WG533; WG553–WG558; WL737–WL759; WL785–WL801; and WR951–WR969. No fewer than 14 squadrons flew them – Nos 37, 38, 42, 120, 203, 204, 205, 206, 210, 220, 224, 228, 240 and 269 – and the Mark was also used by ASWDU and the JASS Flight. (In the course of the Shackleton's long RAF history several squadrons were disbanded or amalgamated, the overall object being to keep in being those with the longest and most distinguished history.)

Although most of the noise and fatigue problems remained in the Mk 2s the changes made the aircraft highly effective and especially versatile as later narratives will prove. The rapid development of the Mk 2 meant that initially a number of squadrons operated both Mk 1As and Mk 2s side by side – a policy dropped in 1954 because of the quite wide differences in operating procedures both in the air and on the ground.

One of the type's greatest assets, applying to all Marks and Phases, was that squadrons or parts of them could set off on long detachments and goodwill tours in a self-contained manner, ground crew flying as passengers and a vast quantity of spares and stores being carried in the fuselage and in bomb bay panniers.

During 1955 and 1956 mid-upper turrets were removed from all the Mk 1 and 2 aircraft, giving more much-needed internal space. The series of Phase modifications eventually brought the interior fits of the

Mk 2s up to the same standard as the almost completely redesigned Mk 3s.

Mk 2s flew in a variety of colour schemes beginning with the grey top and white sides and undersurfaces of the early 1950s. As with the Mk 1s this scheme was followed by dark sea grey with white fuselage tops circa 1955–56. Aircraft of No 205 Squadron, Far East Air Force, also had white bands painted on their upper wing surfaces to assist the cooling of fuel tanks in tropical temperatures. Squadron numbers, painted on fuselage sides, which had replaced fore-and-aft code letters, disappeared circa 1966 with the advent of centralised servicing.

The complaints about noise and fatigue continued to flow in from the squadrons and in the autumn of 1954 the building of Shackleton Mk 2s at Manchester was terminated with the completion of WR969. A complete redesign task was undertaken under Issue 3 of Specification R5/46, to result in Avro Type 716, or Shackleton MR Mk 3.

In October 1954 No 240 Squadron had been detailed to carry out aircrew fatigue trials under the direction of staff of the Institute of Aviation Medicine. Each crew involved flew 60 hours in seven days through the hours

Left:
Many tales are told of culinary experiences in Shackleton galleys – several concerned with exploding tins of soup, others with the fire hazards of leaving dish cloths to dry in the accepted domestic manner.

Above:
Mk 2s of No 224 Squadron. *John Latimer*

Above right:
Mk 2s of No 210 Squadron pictured in June 1964. Note the ventral 'dustbin' radar housings in two different stages of extension.

Right:
A Mk 2 Shackleton, still with dorsal gun turret, taking part in a fly-past over Buckingham Palace in 1956. *MoD*

I was going to cook SOLE VÉRONIQUE: FILLETS OF BEEF À LA POMPADOUR and CHILEAN LECHE NAVADA but I lost the BÉRCHAMEL SAUCE so you'll have to make do with bacon and eggs – again.

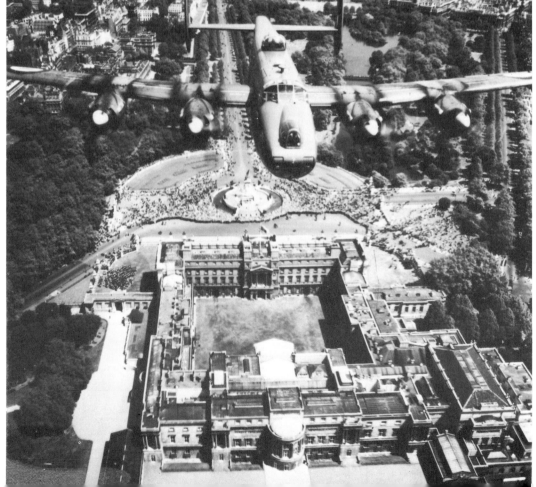

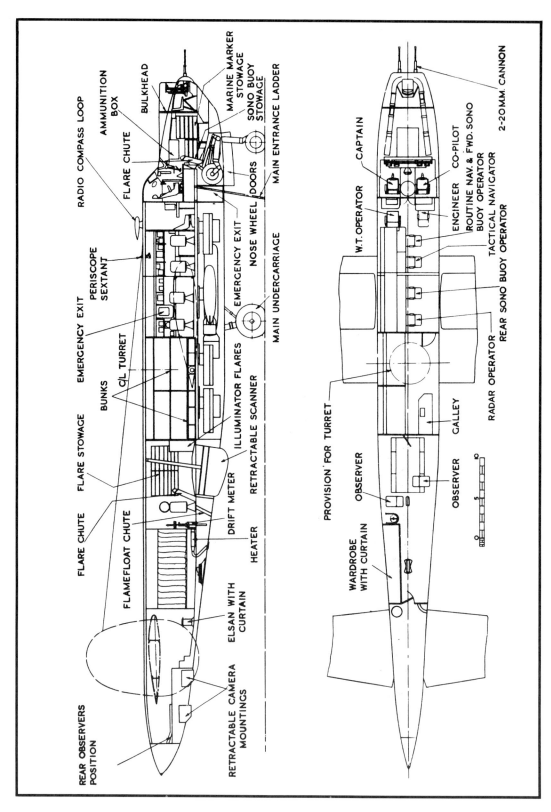

REAR OBSERVERS POSITION

RADIO COMPASS LOOP

AMMUNITION BOX

BULKHEAD

FLARE CHUTE

MARINE MARKER STOWAGE

SONO BUOY STOWAGE

MAIN ENTRANCE LADDER

FLARE CHUTE

FLARE STOWAGE

EMERGENCY EXIT

PERISCOPE SEXTANT

EMERGENCY EXIT

NOSE WHEEL DOORS

MAIN UNDERCARRIAGE

C/L TURRET

BUNKS

ILLUMINATOR FLARES

RETRACTABLE SCANNER

FLAMEFLOAT CHUTE

DRIFT METER

HEATER

ELSAN WITH CURTAIN

RETRACTABLE CAMERA MOUNTINGS

W.T. OPERATOR

CAPTAIN

ENGINEER

CO-PILOT

ROUTINE NAV. & FWD. SONO BUOY OPERATOR

TACTICAL NAVIGATOR

2-20MM. CANNON

PROVISION FOR TURRET

OBSERVER

GALLEY

OBSERVER

RADAR OPERATOR

REAR SONO BUOY OPERATOR

WARDROBE WITH CURTAIN

Above:
**The first prototype Mk 3, WR970, in flight. This aircraft was
lost in the tragic accident referred to in this chapter and later.**
*British Aerospace – picture, taken by Paul Cullerne, then staff
photographer A.V. Roe & Co. Ltd*

Left:
Internal arrangement of Shackleton Mk 3.

of darkness – this amounted to four 15-hour sorties on
alternate days, taking off at 16.30hrs and landing at
07.30hrs the following morning. Each crew member
was given a list of specific tasks and his performance
monitored to determine any loss of efficiency. Medical
checks were carried out to determine weight loss,
changes in eating habits, bowel activity and other
intimate matters. Sqn Ldr (Retd) Denys Swarbrick,
now living in Brixham, Devon, recalls that most crews
lost a considerable amount of weight, became
constipated and found difficulty in resting properly
between flights because of the 'Shackleton buzz' which
went on ringing in their ears long after landing.

The redesign work in the light of such evidence went
on under conditions of some urgency in Manchester.
The basic Shackleton concept had proved itself and
many more aircraft of the type were needed quickly, at
least to replace the last of Coastal Command's still
faithful Sunderlands.

There was another incentive 'in the wings' for A.V.

Roe Ltd to get on with the job: two goodwill visits by
Shackletons of Nos 42 and 204 Squadrons to South
Africa in 1953 and 1955 had resulted in considerable
interest being shown in the type by the South African
Air Force, then as now wanting to watch the Cape of
Good Hope shipping route, and wanting the best
aircraft available with which to do the job. What in fact
turned out to be the only export order for Shackletons
was in the offing.

The past is in the past, but there is a reasonable
amount of evidence available that the South African
government recognised the Shackleton in its Mk 2
form as the sort of aircraft it wanted, but had some
hesitation because of the crew fatigue problems,
undoubtedly mentioned during the goodwill missions
over a 'tube or two' between aircrews. However, it
went ahead to clinch a deal on learning that a much
improved Mk 3 was on the stocks. The eventual South
African purchase of Shackletons, and their use over 27
years, will be recorded in more detail later.

The main differences which emerged in the Mk 3
design were the tricycle/nosewheel undercarriage,
wingtip fuel tanks to put fuel capacity up to 4,248 Imp
gal, a 'wrap-around' clear vision pilots' cockpit screen,
and perhaps most importantly liberal sound-proofing
throughout with a cosy brown-and-cream colour
scheme replacing the depressing black interior of the
earlier Marks, which the Institute of Aviation
Medicine had added to its debit points in its assessment

LEADING PARTICULARS OF SHACKLETON MK 3

Principal Dimensions
Wing span: 119ft 10in
Length: 87ft 4in
Height of fins:* 23ft 4in
Track: 23ft 9in
Tailplane span: 33ft 0in

*When the aircraft is jacked up for scanner functioning tests, the height of the fins above the ground is 24ft 9in.

Basic weight: Approx 64,300lb

Main wheel units
Type: Two forward-retracting twin-wheel units
Shock-absorber struts: Electro-Hydraulic 5039, oleo-pneumatic
Fluid: 34B/9100572, H-515, NATO OM-15
Air pressure (no load): 700lb/sq in
Tyre pressures: 95lb/sq in at 108,000lb; 93lb/sq in at 106,000lb; 87lb/sq in at 100,000lb; 80lb/sqin at 94,000lb; 70lb/sq in at 84,000lb
Brakes: Dunlop hydraulic with maxaret units
Brake operating pressure: 1,500lb/sq in

Nosewheel unit
Type: Backward-retracting twin wheel, steerable
Shock-absorber strut: Dowty, liquid-spring
Fluid: 34B/9100572, H-515, NATO OM-15
Charge pressure (no load): 1,500lb/sq in
Tyre pressures: 101lb/sq in at 108,000lb; 98lb/sq in at 106,000lb; 93lb/sq in at 100,000lb; 90lb/sq in at 94,000lb; 80lb/sq in at 84,000lb

Fuel system
Type of fuel: AVGAS 100/130 (34A/9100444, NATO F-18); Acceptable substitute AVGAS; 115/145 (NATO F-22); Water/methanol fluid (34B/9440428, AL 24).
Pumps: Main tanks: SPE418 Mk 3; Bomb bay tank: FB6 Mk 3; Water/methanol: SPM7.

Tank capacities

	Gallons	Unusable fuel, gallons
No 1:	539	6
No 2:	573	7
No 3:	297	
No 4:	311	3
No 5:	185	
No 6 (tip):	253	5
Total each side:	2,158	21
Bomb bay tank:	400	10
Maximum total capacity:	4,716	52
Water/methanol capacity:	26 each side	

of aircrew fatigue. There were other less clearly identifiable changes. For example, ailerons of greater chord were fitted to improve handling, particularly during the almost aerobatic low-level sorties required at least simulated attacks on submarines, and indeed during very real attacks on dissident tribesmen and the like in the Middle and Far East.

The basic design changes resulting in the Mk 3 put the maximum weight up to 100,000lb. The Royal Air Force, however, wanted still more from its Shackletons – yet more payload to accommodate more equipment for the essential war against the submarine and stronger and heavier nosewheel undercarriage components. Matters proceeded fairly rapidly therefore towards the evolution of the 'ultimate Shackleton' – the Mk 3 Phase 3 version with its

Left:
A Mk 3 of No 201 Squadron on exercise. *MoD*

Below:
Mk 3 No WR970 in flight, displaying some of its 'underneath' features including the lower nose observation/bomb aimer's position, the radome in retracted position and the transparent tail observer's position. *PA-Reuter*

maximum weight up to 108,000lb. This meant that this version had to be assisted off the ground by a pair of jets, at least to enable the type to operate form the 6,000ft runways which were standard at many overseas RAF stations at the time. The Avro sales liteature about the Mk 3 said:

'Strategic considerations now demand an aircraft with a performance which includes the ability to patrol an area, located some 1,000 miles from base, for a period of seven or eight hours.

'In addition to the prime requirements of the anti-submarine role, considerable importance is attached to the need for versatility.'

'The Avro Shackleton is an eminently suitable aircraft for air/sea rescue work, troop carrying, medium altitude bombing and anti-smuggling patrols.'

History was to prove the words of that particular public relations script writer of April 1956.

The MR Mk 3 prototype, WR970, first flew on 2 September 1955. Very unfortunately this aircraft flew into fatal trouble just over a year later. Trials at Boscombe Down with it had displayed some

Above:
A Shackleton Mk 3 off the Needles.
British Aerospace – picture, taken by Paul Cullerne of A.V. Roe Ltd in 1958

Above right:
A Mk 3 of No 201 Squadron. *British Aerospace*

unsatisfactory stalling characteristics, especially with the bomb doors open, and it was returned to A.V. Roe Ltd in November 1956 with suggestions that improved stall warning devices should be fitted. Sqn Ldr Jack Wales, a senior Avro production test pilot and also at the same time the very popular commanding officer of No 613 (City of Manchester) Squadron Royal Auxiliary Air Force, took the aircraft off for stalling tests from Woodford on 7 December 1956. So far as anyone could discover control was lost during an induced stall in cloud, resulting in the aircraft becoming inverted with engines stopped. WR970 crashed on the outskirts of the village of Foolow, Derbyshire with all four aboard killed – Jack Wales himself, Mr George Blake (flight test engineer) and flight test observers Mr Charles O'Neill and Mr Raymond Greenhalgh. The second Shackleton Mk 3 (WR971) did not fly until 1956, thus delaying the entry of this type into RAF service.

A total of 34 Mk 3s of various 'Phases' were built for the RAF under serials WR970–WR990, XF700–XF711 and XF730; and eight Mk 3 Phase 2s were delivered to the South African Air Force from may 1957 onwards.

The ultimate Mk 3 Phase 3 aircraft with the Viper jet-assistance equipment entered service with RAF Nos 42, 120, 201, 203 and 206 Squadrons as well as with

ASWDU, and some Mk 3 Phase 1 and Phase 2 Shackletons entered service with Nos 120, 201, 203, 206 and 220 Squadrons RAF.

Mk 3 Phase 1 aircraft contained an improved version of the basic and all-important radar – ASV 21 sets replacing the ASV 13s. They also included relatively early avionics such as ILS (Instrument Landing System), VHR radio homers, radio/radar altimeters, Doppler navigators and search and rescue homing equipment.

Mk 3 Phase 2 Shackletons were fitted with electronic countermeasures equipment involving the fitting of large aerial assemblies on the fuselage roofs which made them identifiable to astute spotters. Additional avionics in the Phase 2 aircraft included TACAN radio bearing and distance measuring equipment, improved radio compasses and active sonobuoys.

The Phase 3 Shackletons, both Mk 2s and 3s, were to be the mainstay of Coastal Command until its

disbandment and absorption into the newly formed Strike Command shortly before the type's replacement in the MR role by the Nimrod – itself based on the by then fairly venerable Comet design.

'Phase' changes were introduced into existing aircraft over both Marks over a period of years, and in the case of the Mk 3 the additional equipment, plus the weight of the tricycle undercarriage, meant a requirement for more power. The oil feed arrangements in the Griffons were modified and they were styled '58s', but the fundamental change in the Mk3 Phase 3 was the addition of the 'jet assistance' in the form of a Viper underneath and below each outboard main engine. This in turn called for some main spar strengthening.

The addition of the compact but potent Viper jets to the Mk 3 Phase Shackletons posed a number of problems for the engineers at the Coventry factory (which had its origins in Armstrong Siddeleys, went through a period as Bristol Siddeley and is now part of Rolls-Royce). In April 1964 Bristol Siddeley Engines issued to the Ministry of Aviation Brochure MDS 171/3 showing a development programme for the fitting of Viper BSV 11s – an engine type already well proven in such aircraft as the Jet Provost T4 and the Italian Macchi MB326.

The Viper (still in production in an even more advanced form) is a simple jet with a seven-stage axial compressor driven by a single stage turbine. One of the first problems to be overcome involved proving that it could operate on high octane petrol (AVGAS) instead of its normal kerosene to avoid the necessity of carrying two separate fuel systems in the aircraft. This requirement led to some lengthy investigation into the effects of lead deposits on the turbine blades. Tests proved that the sturdy little engine could indeed 'digest' AVGAS but that restrictions would have to be placed on the periods that the engines could be used especially at maximum power.

Since the main intention was to provide additional power for take-off and perhaps for occasional emergency manoeuvres this did not constitute a major problem, restrictions working out at five minutes use at maximum power of 2,700lb, 20 seconds only at overspeed, but with up to a total of four hours per flight permissible at cruising revolutions. In real emergencies the Vipers could be run at any power setting until an oil pressure warning light came on, thus giving pilots a considerable sense of comfort while moving 108,000lb of aircraft in the near aerobatic manoeuvres sometimes called for by anti-submarine warfare tactics.

No one could have been more pleased to have this reserve of power on tap than Flt Lt Michael Bonesio of

No 203 Squadron, his crew of nine and another nine passengers en route from Gibraltar to Ballykelly on 13 December 1967 in WR987. Their aircraft had been taking part in Exercise 'Eagle Eye' from Malta and had been diverted to Cyprus to fly line patrols when the

Left:
The front end of a Mk 3. *British Aerospace*

Right:
The 'office' of a Mk 3. *British Aerospace*

Below left:
Moving back. The wireless operator's and engineer's positions in a Mk 3. *British Aerospace*

Below:
A bit further back. The tactical team (radar) station in the Mk 3. *British Aerospace*

Below right:
The comforts. The 'Wardroom' and rest bunks. *British Aerospace*

Bottom right:
The back 'business end', showing observers' stations and flare stowage. This and the immediately preceding photographs show the internal fit of Mk 3 Shackletons. Very similar arrangements applied in the later Phases of Mk 2 MR aircraft. *British Aerospace*

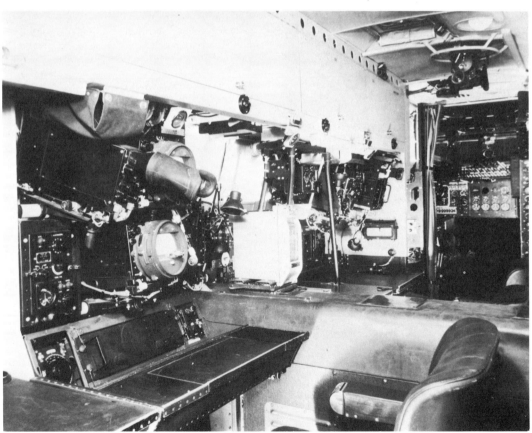

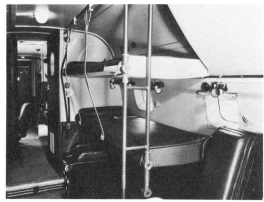

threat of a Turkish invasion was in the air. On the transit flight home they had gone through a severe sandstorm between Malta and Gibraltar and this could be what led to the failure of the translation unit on No 1 engine when they were at 1,000ft and 90 miles northwest of Lisbon. Feathering action was taken on No 1 but the propellers continued to windmill slowly. Wing-tip tank fuel was jettisoned and Lisbon airport informed via a Pan call of the intention to divert and land there.

The Vipers were prepared for immediate start-up – a very wise precaution because 17 minutes later the Flight Engineer reported that No 4 had developed a severe oil leak and would have to be shut down. Fuel jettisoning was stopped, the port Viper started and a Mayday call transmitted. (The jettisoning of high octane fuel at the same time as lighting up a jet engine could obviously have had disastrous consequences).

The crew and passengers were called to ditching stations and No 4 Griffon feathered. Even with the use of take-off power on the remaining two Griffons and 100% power on the port Viper the aircraft lost height but Flt Lt Bondesio was able to hold 500ft at 150kt straight and level. He had to refrain from starting the starboard Viper because it was covered with oil from the leaking No 4 Griffon, thereby presenting a considerable fire risk.

Nursing '987' along with the Viper running at periods of between five and 10 minutes at full power and one-minute 'rests' at 40%, he found he could just make very shallow turns, but even in these his airspeed fell off to a perilous 140kt. Permission was given for a

direct approach on to Runway 03 at Lisbon. Before then the aircraft was hugging the coastline at the entrance to Lisbon Harbour and the crew was map reading its way as the radio compass would not automatic direction find and there was no radar available. Visibility had dropped to 1½ miles in smoke haze from the city and 'it was with some surprise' that the crew saw the Salazar bridge ahead and *above* of them since this relatively new structure was not shown on their maps.

Flt Lt Bondesio turned away from the bridge and flew down the estuary in an unsuccessful effort to gain height. He then managed another very shallow turn to try to pass the bridge on the north side. At this stage he was contacted by the Portuguese Captain of a TAP Boeing 727 who offered assistance. The friendly voice was told of the state of the game and he slowed his jet to match the Shackleton's 140kt, closed in and led the way across the outskirts of the city to the airfield.

Some thermal uplift over the coastline gave '987' a valuable 400ft of height putting it 900ft above mean sea level and 500ft above the airfield. Flt Lt Bondesio saw the runway threshold from two miles and informed the Boeing captain. The latter, with the best will in the world, then descended to the Shackleton's height and

Above:
This group picture, taken of Crew 7 of No 203 squadron while at the Joint Anti-Submarine School in June 1966, includes most of the members of the crew of WR987 aboard at the time of the 'Lisbon Incident' of December 1967. Flg Off (later Flt Lt, later still Maj SAAF) Michael Bondesio is sitting bottom left of picture with the letter 'F' in his hands, which relates to the code letter of the aircraft they flew throughout No 141 JASS Course. The picture was taken at the time when 'Constituted Crews' were created, the intention being that they should as far as possible stay together. Most of this crew did, with the exception of Fl Off Tanner (second from left front row) who obtained captaincy of his own aircraft. The then Sgt, John Latimer, extreme right back row, recalls that there was never any sign of panic aboard, just some bad language on the intercomm when the bridge showed up, which was not marked on their maps. The members of WR987's crew during the 'Lisbon Incident' are: (left-to-right, back row) Sgts Craig, Langan, Briggs, Mapstone and Latimer; (front row) Flg Offs Bondesio, Tanner, Allen, Frazer and Morgans. *John Latimer*

directly ahead, but had to overshoot the runway himself. This manoeuvre meant that '987's' airspeed fluctuated between 140 and 90kt in the Boeing's jetwash. The touchdown was eventually made at 120kt and the aircraft 'brought safely to rest'.

Maj Michael Bondesio SAAF receiving a certificate from Commandant Ralph Hayton, the Commanding Officer of 35 Squadron SAAF, on his completion of 5,000 hours on Shackletons. Maj Bondesio died while at the controls of SAAF Shackleton No 1717 a fortnight after this picture was taken. *No 35 Squadron SAAF via L.J. Vosloo*

The Coastal Command flight safety magazine concluded its report on the incident with the single word 'Phew!!!'

The citation for the well-deserved award of the Air Force Cross to Flt Lt Bondesio read, however:

'Throughout this very serious emergency Flt/Lt Bondesio showed great coolness and presence of mind. For 26 minutes under great strain he fought to keep his heavy and unmanoeuvrable aircraft out of the sea.

'By his superb airmanship and by his courage and determination he brought 19 lives safely through a very perilous predicament and prevented the loss of a valuable operational aircraft.

'He displayed the greatest qualities of leadership and captaincy and his exemplary handling of a very dangerous situation was in accordance with the finest traditions of the Royal Air Force'.

The Coastal Command magazine added that as far was was known it was the first case of a double Griffon engine failure on a Mk 3 Phase 3 Shackleton and had demonstrated that the performance of the aircraft was such that except at very light weight at least one Viper at 100% power was needed to enable height to be maintained. The magazine also went a little further than the official citation by saying that a major accident was averted only through the professional skill of the pilot *and* the competence and discipline of his crew 'who ably supported him throughout the emergency.'

Michael Bondesio later moved his home to South Africa and became a major in the South African Air Force, still flying Shackletons. He died from a heart attack while in his aircraft in 1983 during a patrol off the Namibia coast. Before this tragic event he gave an interview to a South African magazine about the Lisbon incident and said that when he knew he was about to meet up with the Captain of the 727 who had tried hard to help and then baffled him with his landing-abort jet wash he had acquired a bottle of whisky and wasn't sure whether to share it with him or

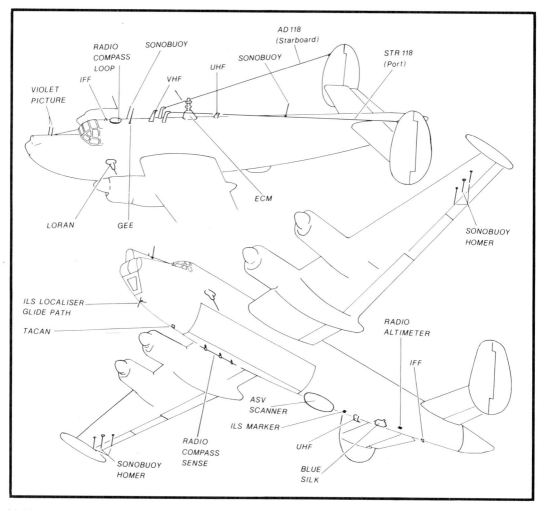

RADIO
COMPASS
LOOP
SONOBUOY
AD 118
(Starboard)
STR 118
(Port)
VIOLET
PICTURE
IFF
VHF
UHF
SONOBUOY
LORAN
GEE
ECM
SONOBUOY
HOMER
ILS LOCALISER
GLIDE PATH
TACAN
RADIO
ALTIMETER
IFF
ASV
SCANNER
ILS MARKER
UHF
SONOBUOY
HOMER
RADIO
COMPASS
SENSE
BLUE
SILK

Above:
Aerial locations on a Mk 3. *British Aerospace*

Right:
Bomb-bay arrangements for anti-submarine Mk 3s.

hit him over the head with it. He decided on the former course.

Some idea of the complexity and the versatility of the Mk 3 Shackleton can perhaps be conveyed by the following information from official document relating to the aircraft. Armament and operational equipment included up to five torpedoes in the bomb bay. Reconnaissance flares (4.5in) could be carried there as well, and a battery of four six-barrelled cartridge flare dischargers was mounted on the starboard side of the fuselage. A twin-cell flare chute in the nose could also be used for the release of markers or sonobuoys.

Up to 32 3½lb flare floats could be carried in the fuselage, plus a selection of other sea markers which could be discharged at the press of a button from both pilots' positions as well as those of the nose gunner, the bomb aimer and anyone who happened to be in the beam and tail lookout positions. Cameras were installed in cupolas at the rear of the fuselage and could be operated by anyone within reach of an appropriate switch. Panniers, later to prove their worth in many an

enterprise, could be carried in the bomb bay, but the official document said, perhaps meaningfully, 'there is no provision for their jettison'.

All these pieces of equipment provided demanding tasks for all 10 members of the average Shackleton crew, not least for the Flight Engineer, whose panel grew larger and larger through the Marks and Phases, and whose check list grew longer and longer, not only during pre-take-off and pre-landing but indeed throughout many an 18, 20 or even 24-hour mission.

Flight Engineers like Master Engineer Ray Donovan, at the time of writing still flying in Shackleton AEW Mk 2s from Lossiemouth, say that there will never again be such a 'trade' in the Royal Air Force once the last 'Shack' goes out of service. Ray

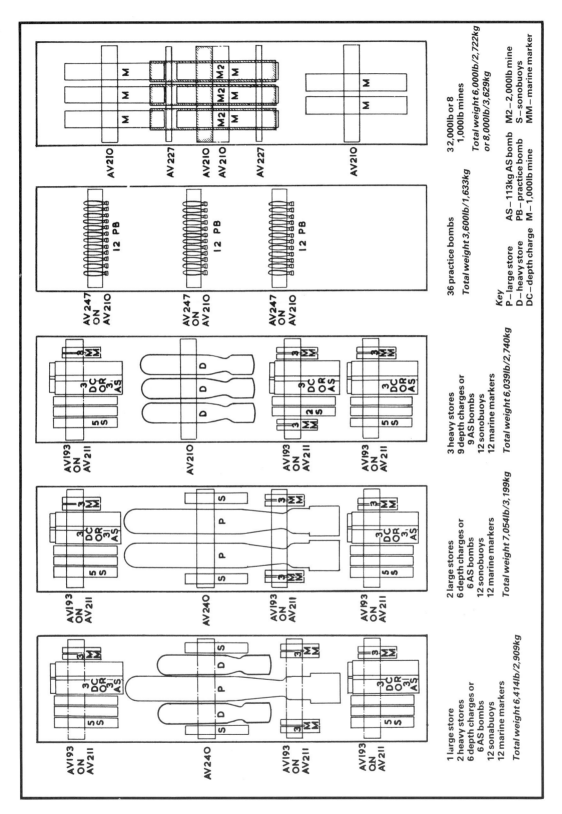

AV193
ON
AV211

1 large store
2 heavy stores
6 depth charges or
6 AS bombs
12 sonabuoys
12 marine markers

Total weight 6,414lb/2,909kg

AV240

AV193
ON
AV211

AV193
ON
AV211

AV193
ON
AV211

AV240

2 large stores
6 depth charges or
6 AS bombs
12 sonobuoys
12 marine markers

Total weight 7,054lb/3,199kg

AV193
ON
AV211

AV193
ON
AV211

AV210

AV193
ON
AV211

AV193
ON
AV211

3 heavy stores
9 depth charges or
9 AS bombs
12 sonobuoys
12 marine markers

Total weight 6,039lb/2,740kg

AV247
ON
AV210

12 PB

AV247
ON
AV210

12 PB

AV247
ON
AV210

12 PB

36 practice bombs
Total weight 3,600lb/1,633kg

AV210

AV227

AV210

AV210

AV227

AV210

32,000lb or 8
1,000lb mines

*Total weight 6,000lb/2,722kg
or 8,000lb/3,629kg*

Key
P – large store   AS – 113kg AS bomb   M2 – 2,000lb mine
D – heavy store   PB – practice bomb   S – sonobuoys
DC – depth charge   M – 1,000lb mine   MM – marine marker

43

Donovan did have a spell on Nimrods but found the Flight Engineer's role on them a little boring – 'a bit like being a chap in shirt-sleeves in an airliner' he described it. He was happy to obtain a transfer back to No 8 Squadron where his skills and talents were not only appreciated but which were very necessary, for example on a Quick Reaction Alert from Lossiemouth with a Mk 2 AEW Shackleton having to be started up and hauled off the ground rapidly, all Griffons running well, in order to detect an approaching Russian 'Bear' and vector some fighters on to it. Ray Donovan was still very happy to be a Master Flight Engineer in a Shackleton in 1984 when this author had the privilege of flying with him in a state of confidence.

As early as October 1961 Air Cdre E.M. ('Teddy') Donaldson, then the Air Forces Correspondent of the *Daily Telegraph* wrote: 'A new proposal is to be studied by the Ministry of Defence to build some 30 Comet 4s, modified for RAF Coastal Command patrol duties to replace the Shackletons which are *now worn out and obsolete!* (Author's italics applied 23 years later!) Air Cdre Donaldson suggested that the proposal was being put forward partly to prevent the RAF from buying the French Breguet Atlantiques to replace the Shackletons. This shrewd airman-cum-journalist was absolutely right in his deductions of the time. He might equally (and may well have) forecast the development of the Nimrod, based on the Comet airframe design, which was quite soon to replace the

Shackleton in the maritime reconnoissance role but which was going to take much, much, longer to usurp it in RAF service altogether.

On 27 November 1969 Coastal Command was formally disbanded at a parade at RAF St Mawgan, Cornwall, The flypast consisted of two Whirlwind SAR helicopters trailing an RAF ensign and a banner showing the Command motto 'Constant Endeavour', followed by a formation of nine Shackletons from the home bases of St Mawgan itself, Ballykelly and Kinloss, and with a single Nimrod Mk 1 bringing up the rear.

The three Shackleton squadrons then still based at Kinloss, Nos 120, 201 and 206, were converted on to Nimrods in 1970. On 1 August that year the MOTU reverted to the title of 236 OCU for Nimrod crew conversion training. The age of the Shackelton, the last of the Roy Chadwick four piston-engined heavies, in RAF service, seemed to be over, but not quite. Not quite by another 15 years at least.

Before outlining the 'interim solution' to the nation's lack of airborne early warning cover which gave the Shackleton another very long lease of life, a development plan which failed, ought to be mentioned for students of the type.

Right:
The successor – at least in the maritime reconnaissance role, but not yet completely – a Nimrod Mk 1. *MoD*

Below:
St Mawgan Shackleton Mk 2s followed by a Nimrod fly in for the Coastal Command disbandment parade and fly-past. *The Times*

Above:
Lincoln SX973 with a Napier Nomad in the nose flying at the Farnboorugh SBAC display in 1951. *British Aerospace*

The desirability of making a maritime reconnaissance aircraft like the Shackleton capable of flying even longer and longer distances was always in designers' and defence politicians' minds. The now sadly defunct company of D. Napier & Son Ltd, Acton, West London, produced a number of highly successful aircraft engines, notably their 'Lions' which powered such stalwarts as the Fairey IIIFs and the record-breaking Fairey Long Range Monoplane. Designers in the company had always been interested in the potential of compression ignition (diesel) engines for aircraft and indeed for other vehicles such as railway locomotives. Their thinking went on towards the combination of a 'diesel front end' and a gas turbine 'back end', the latter portion picking up exhaust gases and pressures from the former part, thus creating a highly effective, low fuel consumption power unit, ideal for such an aeroplane was the Shackleton. The idea inspired some brains at Avro to conceive what might have been a 'Shackleton Mk 4', using the Nomad engine, technically described as a '12-cylinder horizontally opposed, pressure liquid-cooled, two-cycle compression ignition Diesel in-line coupled to an exhaust-driven 11-stage axial flow compressor and turbine assembly'.

One of the development engines, E.125, was fitted to a Lincoln and flown at the Farnborough SBAC display in 1951. Demonstration flights proved that the Lincoln could fly on the single Nomad alone with its four Merlins feathered. A Nomad 2 of more advanced design was proffered by Napiers in 1952 and a trial installation took place the following year when VW131, the second and rather long-suffering Shackleton prototype, was flown into Luton Airport, then Napier's experimental base. Records say that VW131's outer Griffons were removed and 'dummy' Nomads installed to check fitting and mounting arrangements. It is believed that government financial cutbacks stopped the whole programme just as two Nomad 2 engines had been installed for flight tests. It is also sadly recorded that VW131 was shortly afterwards

'reduced to produce' at Luton. Royal Air Force crews of the era, already undertaking 18 and 22-hour missions in Griffon-powered Shackletons, were not entirely disappointed to learn that efforts to increase the aircraft's endurance still further had been thwarted.

At the end of the 1960s, amidst much controversy, a decision was made to phase out large fixed-wing aircraft carriers from the Royal Navy, with HMS *Ark Royal* being the last ship of the type in service. An aspect of that decision which received little attention from the general public was that it would rob the nation of its only airborne early warning capability in the form of the Fleet Air Arm Gannets capable of 'looking over the horizon' with their APS 20 radars, still highly efficient, even though dating back in design from the immediate post-Pearl Harbour days.

An 'interim solution' was produced – the rebuilding and conversion of 12 Mk 2 Phase 3 Shackletons into the AEW role and the basing of them in the north of Scotland from where they could at least look over the horizon from the Iceland-Faroes Gap line. This procedure and the events which followed will be described in more detail in a later chapter. At this stage it need only be recorded that Mk 2 Shackletons serials WL741, WL745, WL747, WL754, WL756, WL757, WL790, WL793, WL795 and WR960, WR963 and WR965 were converted and re-sparred at the former Avro – by then Hawker Siddeley – factories at Bitteswell near Rugby, and Woodford. The conversion process involved a considerable alteration in the profile of the former MR Mk 2s, the radome going back to near the nose but not into the 'chin' position of the Mk 1s. Mk 2 MR aircraft were selected for the conversion because they had suffered less airframe fatigue than the Viper-assisted Mk 3 Phase 3s.

The first conversion to 'Mk 2 AEW' standard (WL745) was test flown from Woodford on 30 September 1971, again by the redoubtable Jimmy Orrell, and on 1 January 1972 No 8 Squadron RAF was re-formed to operate the type. After a 'John Nott' cut in 1981 the strength of the squadron was reduced from 12 to six aircraft but the remaining 'lovely old beasts' were still flying operationally at the time of writing this book.

3
The Primary Role

Few martial arts have seen more rapid development in the 20th century than the war between the submarine and the aircraft. The Shackleton was the 'vehicle' in which many of the weapons now in the hands of the Royal Air Force were tested and proved during the aircraft type's 20 years service in its primary maritime reconnaissance role, a period in which the growth of the Soviet submarine fleet became a major threat to the West.

While the seeking-out and, if necessary, the attacking of surface ships remained a major task for all maritime aircraft, it was the Shackleton's role as a hunter-killer of submarines which called for the greatest effort in terms of the development of equipment and weapons and above all in terms of training.

In the respect of 'hunting' the first step forward from the use of the human eyeball and intelligence acquired from other sources involved the improvement of airborne radar.

As recorded, Mk 1 and 1A Shackletons were equipped with ASV 13 radar sets mounted in a nose radome; this arrangement was rapidly replaced by the ventral 'dustbin' which, apart from eliminating the bird-strike risk, provided for a better 360° scan. The ASV 21 radar fitted to all later Marks and Phases of

Below:
A Mk 2 of No 42 Squadron.

Shackletons was capable of detecting a single submarine periscope given the right conditions and, perhaps more importantly, the right degree of operating skill. The larger 'Schnorkels' of latter-day conventional submarines were regularly detected. The complementary 'close-hunting' device developed and improved during the Shackleton era was the sonobuoy, moving up from non-directional to directional and evolved in both 'passive' and 'active' forms – the latter being faster-acting and more positive but having the disadvantage of being detectable by a hunted, and wily, submarine commander.

Two other important anti-submarine devices were added to the Shackletons' payloads – Magnetic Anomaly Detectors (MAD) working on mine-detector principles, which detect changes in the earth's magnetic field resulting from the presence of a submarine underwater, and an intriguing piece of equipment called 'Autolycus'. This device, referred to in the popular press of the time as the 'sub-sniffer' but properly termed Exhaust Trail Indicator, was claimed to be able to detect changes in the ionisation of particles emitted from the exhaust of a submarine 'snorting' or 'schnorkelling' on the surface for up to 15 miles downwind. Its efficacy was always rather suspect and the predominance of the nuclear submarine lessened the requirement, although its performance was improved in the Mk 3 Phase 3 Shackletons. Its existence is worth permanent record, however, if only to compliment the imagination of the anonymous

coiner of its code-name. Autolycus, as every Shakespearian scholar knows, was 'the snapper-up of unconsidered trifles' in *Winter's Tale*.

On the weapons side the advance of technology moved rather more slowly, several basic and well proven World War 2 types remaining as main armament throughout most of the type's maritime reconnaissance career. The weapons carried in the bomb bay could consist of various mixes of practice or lethal HE bombs, Mk 30 or Mk 44 (homing) torpedoes and Mk 11 depth charges. Provision was also made for mine-laying with alternative loads of 2,000-pounders and 1,000 pounders.

Happily for the world at large the Shackletons never had to carry out 'in anger' their ultimate primary role – that of killing an enemy submarine. Nevertheless in any record of their primary role it has to remembered that aircraft of No 38 Squadron provided full anti-submarine cover for the invasion fleet during the Suez operation.

Although the tail turrets disappeared at an early stage and the mid-uppers were progressively removed, the twin 20mm cannon in the nose were retained. It had been noted that potential enemy submarines no longer carried deck-mounted quick-firers and that the 'duels' of World War 2 were unlikely to be repeated. The retention of the nose armament was however to prove of considerable value in the colonial policing role.

Above:
Ship surveillance.

The finding, recording and 'discouragement' of hundreds of surface vessels bent on piracy, gun-running and the putting of landing parties ashore during several of the Middle and Far East conflicts could of course be regarded as primary role tasks even, though they were strictly speaking under the umbrella of colonial policing. So could the spotting and recording of Soviet ship movements in the Atlantic and its Eastern Approaches under so-called exercise conditions by the UK-based Shackleton squadrons.

On the matter of attacks upon submarines former Sergeant Signaller 'Dinty' More does recall an episode during a joint service exercise when he and his crew returned to Ballykelly full of pride at having located a sub, straddled it with small, noisy but non-lethal bombs and photographed the scene, only to be told by the Royal Navy de-briefers that they had had no such vessel within 100 miles of the position recorded. Mr More recalls the photographs being produced and bent over, and the de-briefing session at HMS *Sea Eagle* (JASS) taking on a distinctly added air of significance. He thinks that happily for all concerned the Soviet submarine so rudely interrupted in the course of whatever it was doing was proved to have been in Norwegian territorial waters, so that the incident did not become an international one. 'One of those "veils

of silence" seemed to descend upon the whole episode', he told me.

The training demands on the Shackleton air and ground crews and on the aeroplanes themselves during the 1950s and 1960s in fact fell little short of those of wartime. Coastal Command's responsibilities to NATO in the Atlantic were enormous and with the Soviet submarine and surface ship threat growing yearly the phrase '*Operational* Flying Exercise' had a significant ring about it. In a sense the training was for real since it combined with it constant vigilance over potential enemy ship movements. The same applied to the training carried out in the Middle and Far East, much of which had to be interspersed with the minor war secondary role tasks; the resident Shackleton squadrons at such bases as Gibraltar, Malta, Aden, Sharjah and Singapore were frequently being reinforced by aircraft on detachment from the UK.

The bases in the north of Scotland, Northern Ireland and Cornwall were well chosen because the primary task in the event of war would have been the killing of nuclear submarines on their way out to firing positions, plus of course the destruction of conventional vessels wherever they might be. Perhaps partly because of the remoteness and therefore the self-contained nature of these bases, partly because of the sharing of some fairly considerable discomforts if not actual hardship, and partly the teamwork and leadership involved in operating a 'big crew' aircraft, a remarkable degree of morale built up in the 'Shackleton world'. A typical

'OFE' (Operational Flying Exercise) could involve an outward transit of about 1,000 miles taking some six hours, a similar period flying patterns in a search area and another six-hour return cruise, often with a little surprise sprung by the exercise controllers at the end of it in case anyone was relaxing too much. That plus briefing and de-briefing could fill an airman's 24-hour day.

The broad principles employed for the seeking out of a target involved first the use of intelligence from surface ships and other sources, then medium-distance radar and human eyeball searches, finally precise location with sonobuoys.

Among the many training devices used were ASTIs (Anti-Submarine Training Indicators) consisting of flame and smoke floats released by co-operating exercise submarines.

The navigators usually controlled weapon selections from the bomb bay – torpedoes, depth charges, bombs, flares, or sonobuoys – and released them from the lower nose bomb-aimers position. It was, however, usually the pilots' prerogative to finalise visual depth charge attacks. A good attack could deliver six depth charges from 100ft altitude in well under four minutes. Some crews recall that the sight of their signallers dropping flares amidst clouds of smoke at the back end and reflected glare, was reminiscent of the gun deck of HMS *Victory* at Trafalgar.

Most of the flying was at low level, even transit 'cruises' being at no more than a few thousand feet, and in winter over the Atlantic or the Irish and North Seas this usually meant a rough ride most of the way with the regular supply of hot drinks and food a matter of great importance to all. Perhaps surprisingly, many aircrews who have served in both types prefer the Shackleton's fairly easy motion, with gently flexing wings, to that of the harder ride of the Nimrod in turbulence.

For many years simulated attacks on submarines or target devices representing them were carried out from 100ft by day and 200ft by night, but for a number of good reasons the night attack height was lifted to 500ft. One of the good reasons, and a fair example of the general arduousness of MR training, was the memorable experience in April 1961 of the crew of WR957 of No 204 Squadron from Ballykelly.

Towards the end of a long Atlantic sortie the crew were required to carry out a night bombing attack on a

Left:
A typical ship identification photograph. *David Guthrie*

Right:
Former Shackleton Sergeant Signaller (later Master AEOp) Alister 'Dinty' More AFC.

Below and below right:
Periscope, schnorkel and bursting practice bomb from Shackleton. *both David Guthrie*

Above and left:
Interior scene. *both The Times.*

Above right:
Interior scene. The engineers' panel is on the right.
The Times.

Right:
Navigator at work. Described as 'a rare scene'. *J.G. Marsden.*

buoy target off the Donegal coast and it was a dark and dirty night indeed. The aircraft captain was the then Flt Lt Bill Houldsworth (later well known to the aviation world as one of the pilots of the Memorial Flight Lancaster *City of Lincoln*) and he made a standard radar approach at about 1,000ft followed by descent to 300ft with sodium flares discharged to illuminate the rather small target. A combination of flying spray and back glare from the flares robbed his bomb aimer of a clear view at the last moment and Bill Houldsworth lifted his head momentarily to give some final guidance, lowered it again to see his altimeter needle under the 50ft mark. He and his co-pilot, now Sqn Ldr (Retd) Bill Howard, recall very vividly what they described in their report as 'a heavy impact' as they pulled back jointly on the yokes followed by some interesting conversation on the intercom during the climb away.

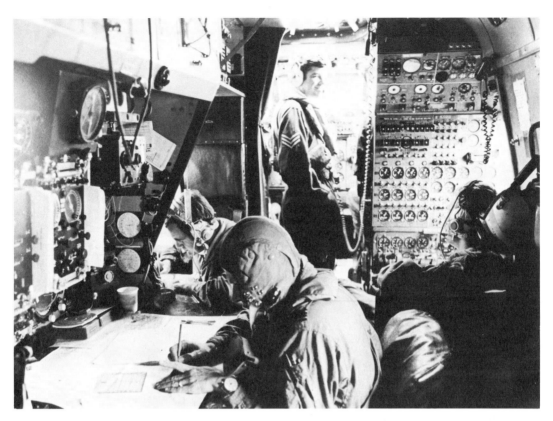

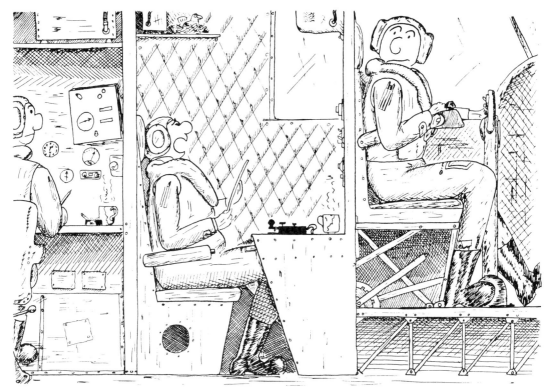

MESSAGE READS - MERRY CHRISTMAS, REMAIN AIRBORNE A FURTHER TEN HOURS

Bill Howard, who went on flying Shackletons into their AEW phase at Lossiemouth and still flies civilian charter aircraft in the North of Scotland, has a very distinct memory of the unruffled voice of a sergeant radar operator possessed of cool nerves, a dry sense of humour and an Ulster accent (attributes which often go together), who first reported that his picture had disappeared off the screen and a few seconds later that it was no wonder because the radome and the scanner had also disappeared. Another report came from the tail cone to the effect that it had a lot of sea water in it.

Left:
This self explanatory cartoon and the two others included in the book are culled from *Coastal Through the Looking Glass,* **a volume compiled in the mid-1960s. It has not been possible to establish the name of the artist with certainty, but they are believed to be the work of a former Fl Off David Sheringham. Note fresh egg supply system top centre.** *Cartoons courtesy John Latimer*

Below left:
Friendly coast ahead. Approaching Aldergrove over Malin Head, Northern Ireland after an 'LROFE' – Long Range Operational Flying Exercise. *J.G. Marsden.*

Right:
Flt Lt (later Sqn Ldr) Bill Houldsworth.

Below:
What was left of Bill Houldsworth's radome. *MoD*

They returned to Ballykelly and circled the field until daylight when ground observers were able to tell them that everything necessary for a safe landing still seemed to be there and they duly made one. The damage recorded included the lost radar housing and its contents, two tail cameras and their mountings missing, the tailwheel doors torn off and the main bomb doors bent. Bill Houldsworth, who retired last year (1984), recalls that someone did 'slap the back of his hand' but nothing worse, and confidence in the Shackleton was enhanced still further. Bill Howard wrote afterwards: 'We had survived a near catastrophic incident. The impact had occurred at about 180kts. The resulting damage was spectacular and extensive but "the old grey lady" had ridden through it, shaken herself and carried on regardless.'

Training exercises were of course held at various levels from individual aircraft sortie up to combined British Fleet and NATO schemes, the latter often involving close and distant convoy escort work. Code phrases such as CASEX meaning 'Co-ordinated Anti-Submarine Exercise' and OCEANEX, meaning something similar but bigger and better, entered the language of the MR Shackleton crews and an organisation called JASS became an important part of their lives.

The Joint Anti-Submarine School had been established at HMS *Sea Eagle* on the southern bank of the Foyle just outside Londonderry in the immediate postwar years as a logical successor to the operational base there which had played a major part in the Battle of the Atlantic. All the UK-based Shackleton crews spent at least three weeks a year doing JASS exercises, their aircraft based either at Ballykelly, just up the road, or at Aldergrove (later to become Northern Ireland's civil airport) just down the road.

Left:
NATO co-operation. A Mk 2 of No 204 Squadron and USS *Independence*. *The Times*

Below:
A Mk 3, probably Phase 2, of No 206 Squadron, circa 1965. *courtesy John Latimer*

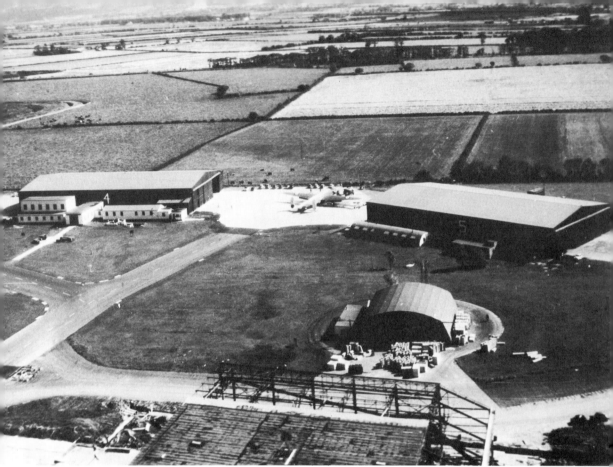

Left:
Ballykelly, commonly known as 'BK', in 1964. *David Hill.*

Below left:
Interior of the 'new' hangar at Ballykelly in 1965. *David Hill*

Above:
Things sometimes went wrong at 'BK'. This aircraft is believed to have attempted to take off with elevator locks in. *J.G. Marsden.*

Below:
Mk 2 Phase 3 WR956 about to be towed away to the fire dump at Ballykelly after severe damage in a landing accident in 1968. *David Hill*

In the Shackleton world Ballykelly will always have a special place of memory. There was the matter of the main Belfast-Londonderry railway line running through the middle of the field with signal bells repeated in the control tower and priority normally given to trains over aircraft; this sometimes resulted in a tired crew having to do a circuit or three at the end of a 20-hour Atlantic exercise until the express had gone by.

There were occasionally some minor disciplinary problems involving NCO aircrews who did not always appreciate the Royal Navy's traditions at *Sea Eagle,*

Above:
Lowering the Ensign for the last time at RAF Ballykelly in 1971. *David Hill*

Left:
'Shackleton Barracks' 1984. The guards in foreground are members of the 1st Battalion Royal Regiment of Fusiliers. The airfield is the permanent home of the 5th (County of Londonderry) Battalion of the Ulster Defence Regiment which shares it with a regular infantry battalion on a two-year tour of duty. The airfield can be seen in the background. *British Army Public Relations Northern Ireland*

Above right:
Mk 2s of No 224 Squadron bombing up at Gibraltar.

Right:
No additional caption necessary, really!

one of these resulting in a Sergeant Signaller claiming that he had 'rowed himself ashore' when the gate was officially closed because 'The Liberty Boat' was not due for another half-hour.

During the 1952–71 period RAF Ballykelly housed at one time or another almost every UK-based Shackleton squadron plus detachments from those of the Middle and Far East Air Forces. The phrase 'Ballykelly Wing' was adopted. A great many friendships were made in the area and in recent years there has therefore been much sadness in the former

IT APPEARS THAT WE ARE LOST AGAIN

'Shackleton world' about the turn of events in that corner of the world. The Royal Air Force took it as a distinct compliment when the British Army, on taking over the base at an early stage of the current troubles, named it 'Shackleton Barracks'. The IRA bombing of the 'Drop in Well' pub just outside the main gate, which held so many happy memories for so many former and present members of the RAF, brought particular pain over a very long range.

A great deal went right for the Shackleton squadrons during their long periods of training from Ballykelly and Aldergrove: understandably a few things went wrong too, and after a lapse of some 15 years it might not be improper to record some of them. The sources of some of the stories had better remain anonymous – it is possible that some have improved in the telling – but the author has no reason to doubt their basic accuracy and they do add to the folklore of an aeroplane which has gained so much affection.

There was, it appears, an occasion during a major NATO exercise when a Signaller took a heavily encoded message which, acccording to whether he had got one slightly garbled letter right or not, meant that the crew should fly from St Eval back to Ballykelly, or alternatively proceed to Jacksonville USA. Under one-way transmission radio silence rules imposed for the exercise he was not allowed to ask for a 'say again' and opted for Jacksonville in his intercom message to the Captain. He recalls that the length of his fingernails was shortened at refuelling stops where fuel was provided but some surprise expressed at their appearance, but that he finally saw a future for himself in the RAF beyond sanitary duties when members of the USN greeted the crew with a supply of hot climate clothing at Jacksonville and congratulated them on their navigation prowess.

There was also, it is said, the occasion when an all-NCO Shackleton crew detailed at short notice for a NATO exercise in the Atlantic expressed among themselves over the intercomm some displeasure at the standards of behaviour of their American allies. This commentary reached something of a peak when, on receiving no reply from a control tower for take-off clearance, the Flight Sergeant captain called out (words to the effect of): 'Oh never mind. Give us take-off boost on all four, Engineer, kick me in the posterior and off we will all jolly well go again.' (That is of course a polite translation.) Unfortunately the intercomm system was being broadcast over the main radio output and heard by a number of very senior officers monitoring the exercise, including their own Group Captain.

4
Alternative Roles

The description alternative roles rather than secondary roles would be a far more appropriate one to use for the multifarious tasks undertaken by Shackletons, apart from the pure maritime reconnaissance one – there was certainly nothing secondary even less 'second-class' about any of them. Because so many of these tasks overlapped one another in time scales it will probably be easier to read about them under subject headings rather than in any sort of chronological order: the alternative roles will therefore be catalogued in this chapter under sub-headings.

Colonial Policing: Middle East

Shackletons entered service with Nos 37, 38, 42, 203, 224 and 228 Squadrons, with Mediterranean and Middle East 'homes', between the 1950s and the early 1960s. During this period, in very simple terms, Eastern-bloc aligned nations and other interested parties were trying to thrust their way southwards by various means from the Soviet mainland, down the line of the Red Sea towards the Indian Ocean. This overall policy manifested itself in a series of 'minor wars' in the Yemen/Aden Protectorate and Persian (later 'Arabian') Gulf areas. Shackletons were to become deeply involved.

The original techniques of colonial policing by air had been involved in the 1920s and 1930s by the RAF on the North West Frontier, in what was then called Mesopotamia, and some other arid places under the King's Writ. The tactics used by Middle East Air Force Shackletons bore a marked resemblance to those evolved by such smaller predecessors as Westland Wapitis and Hawker Harts and Audaxes. They consisted of first warning, then frightening a little, and finally if necessary attacking – all the time assisting ground forces to complete the policing task, and all the time trying to keep the loss of human life to a minimum. The principal theatre of such operations was the then Western Aden Protectorate which terminated at its southern end in Aden Colony, and had a substantial British garrison including that at RAF Khormaksar. For many good reasons the British support given to the locally recruited Aden levies was primarily an RAF responsibility, although of course British Army, Royal Navy and Royal Marine units frequently became heavily involved.

Shackletons were in the forefront of many Kiplingesque actions against dissident tribesmen encouraged by the Communist-aligned South Yemen Republic. The Near and Middle East Air Force squadrons were often reinforced by detachments from others based in the UK under Coastal Command, and other operations were mounted from Sharjah in the Persian Gulf to deal with problems which arose in

Below:
No 38 Squadron ground crew in June 1961. *Brian Coomber*

Kuwait and the state of Muscat and Oman. One of the Gulf operations was claimed to include the first occasion during which bombers went into action under the air traffic control of a civil airport, Bahrein.

No 42 Squadron claimed that the first time a Shackleton used any of its weapons 'in anger' was on 13 January 1957 when one of its aircraft, acting in the Air Observation Post role (yet another example of its versatility) was directed by ground forces on to a band of dissident tribesmen in the Beihan area near the Yemen frontier, and strafed them with its nose cannon. The usual technique employed by the Shackletons and other aircraft was, as in North West Frontier days, first to drop leaflets inviting dissidents to surrender 'or else'; then, if there was no response, drop some more saying that their village would be bombed at an advertised hour to give the women and children especially the opportunity to move to open ground or take cover. The third stage involved actual bombing with anything from 20lb fragmentation

Above:
Mk 2 WL796 over the Western Aden Protectorate in 1958. *Jim Simpson*

Above right:
Mk 2 WR966 of No 37 Squadron over Venoms of No 8 Squadron at Khormaksar, Aden in 1959. *Jim Simpson*

'frighteners' to 1,000-pounders – the latter in fact causing remarkably little damage to mud and straw buildings in the event of anything short of a direct hit.

Although the loss of human life was thought to be relatively low during this sort of operation a number of goats and camels inevitably succumbed to the misfortunes of war. A story is told (and verified from several sources even if not appearing in published records) of an occasion when a Shackleton was carrying out a coup de grace strafing run with its twin 20mm cannon on an apparently empty village when a stray camel ran across the line of fire. To the nose

gunner's astonishment the camel exploded with a considerable tongue of flame and a cloud of smoke. The general line of conversation on the intercomm was 'Whatever will they think of next?', but on return to Khormaksar an intelligence officer preferred the logical explanation. It was, he said, the practice of certain dissidents to mix ammunition and explosives with camel feed, take them through checkpoints and then recover the contraband in the due course of nature. One raconteur of this story said that the gunner, who was something of an animal lover, had suffered quite severe shock. Members of his audience suggested that the trauma must have been rather worse for the camel.

The total tonnage of bombs dropped reached formidable figures – No 37 alone accounting for 400,000lb worth during April 1958 when actions against dissidents attempting to cut the Dhala trade route reached wartime proportions.

All the Middle East operations were carried out in difficult climatic conditions. For the ground crews temperatures inside fuselages sometimes reached 140° Fahrenheit and for aircrews the mountainous terrain, heat and humidity produced turbulent air conditions at low level which made for hazardous flying not to mention discomfort to the most hardened stomachs. Towels to wipe off perspiration even while airborne formed an essential part of flying equipment.

Throughout the Middle East campaigns Shackletons were frequently diverted to search and rescue tasks and were often called on to provide top cover for single engine aircraft in transit over the sea and over 'empty quarters'. From 1957 onwards the re-equipment of the Coastal Command squadrons with Mk 3s meant that the Middle and Far East units could be fully equipped with Mk 2s, which were in many ways the most suitable of all the variants. In spite of the demanding and hazardous nature of the Middle East operations no Shackletons were lost, although the engineering branch had plenty of servicing and repair problems.

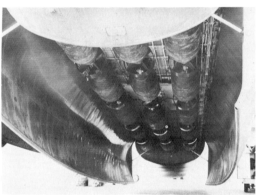

Colonial Policing: Far East

Although the Shackleton went into service too late to participate in the Korean War of 1950–53 or in the earlier phases of the long drawn-out Malayan Emergency, Mk 1s and 2s mainly operated by No 205 Squadron 'Out of Singapore' were operational in the important anti-piracy role well before the next major flare-up in the Far East occurred in the form of the Borneo Confrontation between 1962 and 1966. As listed later in the melancholy, but necessary, crashes and losses chapter, a Mk 1 of No 205 Squadron was lost with 11 lives on such an operation, combined with a rescue task, when flying from Labuan Island, a base later to become of great significance.

No 205 Squadron was quickly into action with its Mk 2 Shackletons after the Communist-backed rebel leader Azahari attempted to seize the Seria oilfields in the State of Brunei (then part of the British-protected northern coast and hinterland of the large island of Borneo) on 8 December 1962. Amongst an armada of

Top:
Bombing up WR556 of No 37 Squadron, Aden 1958.
Jim Simpson

Above left:
Thousand-pounders in the bomb bay, Aden. *Jim Simpson*

Above:
20lb practice or 'frighteners'. *Jim Simpson*

Above right:
A load of 25 500-pounders. *Jim Simpson*

Right:
The last crews of No 205 Squadron to leave the Far East in 1972. *MoD*

aircraft of different types which was hastily assembled in Singapore for what turned out to be a highly successful ad hoc rapid reinforcement operation, No 205 Squadron's Shackletons carried out 15 round trips

Above:
The last Shackleton of No 205 Squadron on its way home from the Far East in 1972. This picture was taken over the Mediterranean from a United States Navy Phantom off USS *Enterprise*. The aircraft was bearing a precious object – see Chapter 6. *US Navy*

Right:
Malayan scene. *Sqn Ldr Bill Howard*

between Singapore and Brunei, each amounting to about 1,200 miles, carrying troops and heavy equipment. One great asset of the Shackletons to the overstretched logistics experts was their ability to make the round trips without intermediate refuelling.

Throughout the Borneo Confrontation No 205 Squadron, often supported by Nos 203 and 204, carried out continuous long range (in effect primary role) tasks, patrolling coastlines and spotting and recording the shipping movements of the then 'enemy' Communist-aligned Indonesian Government. Vessels of all shapes and sizes suspected of bringing weapons and landing parties to the coasts of North Borneo, Sabah, Brunei and Sarawak, and sometimes to the East coast of the Malayan peninsula itself, were tracked, identified, and then usually 'discouraged' by surface ships of the Royal and Commonwealth navies homed on to them by the Shackletons. Sorties specifically designed to prevent infiltration on to the Malayan Peninsula were code-named 'Hawkmoth', and in November 1964 alone No 205 Squadron logged one 'Sverdlov' class cruiser and two 'Skory' class destroyers of Russian origin.

Numerous search and rescue tasks were also carried out by the Shackletons based at Changi (Singapore), Kai Tak (Hong Kong), Labuan Island and sometimes at Gan, the RAF's mid-Indian Ocean coral atoll staging post which played such a significant part in all the British Far East operations until the final withdrawal in 1971.

As in the Middle East Shackletons were frequently employed to act as top cover for single-engined fighter and other aircraft required to transit over vast stretches of open sea, and numerous 'live' search and rescue missions were flown. On one notable occasion in April 1964 an Indonesian submarine was located, tracked and eventually persuaded to turn back from whatever was its nefarious mission in the South China Sea. It was in fact first spotted by an ever alert and awake No 205 squadron navigator, Flt Lt J. Dryburgh, who at the time was travelling as a passenger in a Hastings between Labuan and Singapore. Good inter-Service radio communications resulted in HMS *Lincoln* persuading the captain of Indonesian Navy submarine No 408 to alter course for home.

As in the Middle East the climatic conditions made for hard and uncomfortable work by both ground and air crews of the Shackletons. Average temperatures were between 88° and 90° Fahrenheit with extremely high humidity and up to 3in of rainfall a day, often much more at Borneo bases such as Labuan Island.

After the agreement between the recently created nation of Malaysia and Indonesia ending the 'Confrontation' on 13 August 1966, No 205 Squadron and its supporters reverted to peacetime duties, still involving anti-piracy patrols which if anything tended to increase in necessity in Far Eastern waters once open warfare had ceased.

No 205 Squadron and its Shackletons returned to the United Kingdom in 1971 for disbandment.

The Beira Patrol

At an early stage of the Rhodesian independence crisis of the mid-1960s, HM Government of the time imposed an embago on oil supplies entering the country via Mozambique and charged the Royal Navy and the Royal Air Force with the task of enforcing it – or at least attempting so to do. This led to what was in essence a primary role task for numerous Shackleton squadrons which sent detachments for two-month tours to a primitive airfield called Majunga in the island Republic of Malagasy (formerly Madagascar) in order to maintain round-the-clock patrols over the Mozambique Channel and beyond.

The task again presented many challenges for both ground and air crews. Conditions at Majunga were distinctly uncomfortable, not to say primitive, and many difficulties were encountered in obtaining spare parts and other essential supplies. At one stage, because of the lack of towing tractors (rather essential if a Shackleton wandered off the runway on to some very wet and boggy ground) a locally owned steam roller was requisitioned and apparently performed very well – providing the fire had been lit below its boiler by the first-light stand-by ground crew.

In the air the patrols were long and wearisome, the normal procedure being for the Shackletons to spot and identify suspect tankers and then direct RN ships to close with them. 'The watch' was maintained

without loss of aircraft although weather conditions sometimes made the task hazardous. The now Group Captain David Leppard RAF recalls flying his Mk 2 Shackleton on the Beira Patrol into a 'revolving tropical storm' with a 70 millibar drop on the barometer and winds gusting up to 140kt. He, his crew, and the aeroplane all survived but he estimates that it put about 2½ years fatigue life on the airframe and reduced the life expectancy of himself and his crew by roughly the same amount.

Trooping

Shackletons were used for ad hoc trooping movements on numerous occasions during the Middle and Far East conflicts including the rapid reinforcement operation at the commencement of the Borneo Confrontation, but one of their biggest operations in this role was during the Suez affair of 1956. Under the general code-name of 'Encompass' five aircraft of No 206 Squadron airlifted the 16th Parachute Brigade from Blackbushe to Cyprus as an exercise in 1956. Earlier trials had proved that a Shackleton could carry 33 fully-armed soldiers, with their heavy kit in the bomb bay panniers. The conclusion of this 'exercise' coincided with 'Encompass' becoming a full military operation – in

Below:
The Saro airborne lifeboat, first conceived in design by Uffa Fox, was fitted to prototype Shackletons and tested. This arrangement, as in South Africa, was discarded at an early stage in favour of the much more efficient Lindholme Gear. This picture shows an early Mk 1 fitted with Airborne Lifeboat No 801. *British Aerospace*

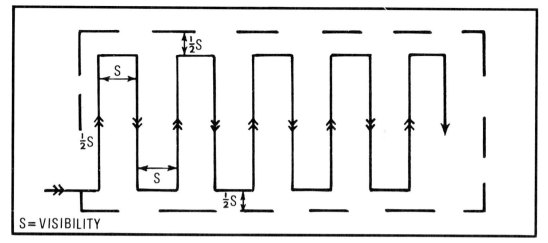

S = VISIBILITY

Left:
A Mk 2 Shackleton, probably a prototype, being demonstrated at a Farnborough SBAC display fitted with Airborne Lifeboat No 804. *British Aerospace*

Below left:
Close-up of airborne lifeboat fitting. *British Aerospace*

Above:
Creeping Line Ahead search pattern.

Right:
Expanding Square search pattern.

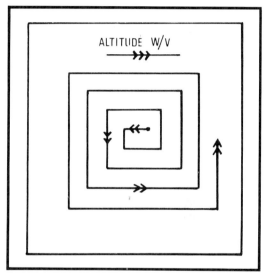

ALTITUDE W/V

the Suez war – and other Shackletons flew Bomber Command personnel and troops out to bases in Cyprus and Malta. At the end of this rather ill-fated (but militarily successful) campaign Shackletons of Nos 204, 228 and other squadrons lifted the 1st and 3rd Battalions of the Parachute Regiment as well as the whole of the Headquarters of 16 Independent Parachute Brigade Group back to the UK from Cyprus via Idris. (The latter operation was in effect a small-scale version of Operation 'Dodge', carried out 12 years earlier by Lancasters, in which 100,000 'time-expired-men' of the Central Mediterranean Forces, most of them 8th Army veterans who had been away from home for four years without leave, were air-lifted home in seven hours compared with their three-month outward troopship voyages, only one aircraft, its crew and passengers being lost.) Similar seating arrangements were made in the 'Encompass' Shackletons to those in the 'Dodge' Lancasters – encircled numbers painted on the fuselage floors upon which the soldier passengers first deposited their small kit and then squatted on top of it. (The author writes with feeling, having been an appreciative 'Dodge' passenger in 1945.)

Search and Rescue
Until the advent of medium radius (200 miles-plus) twin-engined rescue helicopters in the UK towards the end of the 1960s, Shackletons and their Nimrod successors were the prime-movers in air-sea rescue (by then re-styled 'search and rescue') operations at anything over 50 miles from land. They were needed in similar circumstances elsewhere in the world wherever the Royal Air Force operated. Even when incidents were within the 50-mile offshore radius of the early Sycamore and Whirlwind rescue helicopters Shackletons were called on to provide top-cover for these valiant, but single-engined rotary winged aircraft and there were many joint operations under the cheerful callsigns of 'Playmate' and 'Pedro'. In the opinion of many search and rescue experts the Shackleton was (and still is) superior to the Nimrod in the visual search role with its downward-view positions at nose and tail as well as bubble windows in the beam, and its ability to fly low and slow in the worst of weather.

Search and rescue operations by maritime reconnaissance aircraft usually begin with the drawing

in of information through the many communications channels available from initial Mayday messages and other sources, followed probably by long and arduous 'creeping line ahead', 'expanding square' or 'clover leaf' search pattern flying. This type of task at low level, in the sort of weather that usually accompanies rescue tasks and with quite a lot of 'G' being pulled during frequent 180° turns, can be demanding on both crews and the aircraft. There is also a special sort of strain on the crew members employed as 'eyes', perhaps trying to detect the white hull of a capsized boat in a mass of wave-tops. In the UK it has been normal practice for each MR squadron to be placed on quick reaction SAR standby for a week at a time. In addition any airborne MR aircraft (and in recent years any AEW Shackleton from No 8 Squadron) can be diverted from its task.

Although in recent years helicopters have frequently carried out the final task of picking up survivors, many incidents still occur 'outwith' the range of the biggest of them and Shackletons in their heyday were frequently able to give direct help by dropping equipment, particularly 'Lindholme Gear' which fairly soon after World War 2 was found superior to the airborne lifeboat.

Lindholme Gear, named after the South Yorkshire RAF station where it was invented, consists of three units linked by floating rope giving a spacing of about 200yd between the first and centre unit, and 400yd between the centre and third. The large centre unit normally consists of an MS 9 liferaft, capable of accommodating nine people with numerous survival aids aboard including fresh water, food, first-aid equipment, a homing beacon, tropical or Arctic fishing equipment, a 'de-salter' and such morale builders as cigarettes, seasickness pills and playing cards. The two smaller containers are packed with other stores, some of them dependent on climate.

The objective is to drop the gear in such a way that the floating ropes 'wrap themselves around' the survivors so that little or no physical effort is required on their part. This calls for precise flying at low level, careful planning and frequent practice. In some conditions the gear may drift or be blown down-tide or down-wind on to the survivors; more commonly those in a small liferaft or even alone in a lifejacket wil be driven towards the gear. An assessment of tide, wind and wave conditions has first to be made, usually assisted by the dropping of smoke floats. At night a flare path may also have to be laid first. Final drops are usually made from 160ft at about 140kt.

Although it all sounds simple – and the part played by MR aircraft in rescues is often dismissed in a few laconic lines by newspapers compared to the publicity given to the helicopters – it *can* go wrong. At least two crews recall the disconcerting effect of an MS 9 liferaft inflating prematurely while still attached to the aircraft on a static line. The subsequent events were a drop in airspeed, a call from the tail cone 'We are being followed', and then some emergency cutting action.

The other important role which often falls to MR aircraft is that of acting as 'On Scene Commander'. It can often happen that during a complex rescue the captain of a Shackleton (or nowadays more often a Nimrod), with his overall view, ability to stay overhead for a long period and wide range of communications, is in the best position to co-ordinate the efforts of other aircraft and surface vessels. This can result in a relatively junior RAF officer taking on a very heavy responsibility and offering suggestions (if not actual orders) to those from other services (and indeed nations), far senior to himself. Search and rescue operations and training of course involve much co-operative work not only with helicopters but with the RNLI and indeed any surface ships in a position to help.

A particularly important role in the 1950s–1960s was the escorting-in of the piston-engined airliners and bombers of the era which not all that infrequently developed problems in mid-Atlantic or over other ocean spaces. As old hands like 'Dinty' More recall, this requirement could sometimes be frustrating. They would take off from Ballykelly, plough their way into the prevailing southwesterlies to rendezvous with say a Constellation with one engine out which would then proceed to Shannon at a considerably faster rate and higher altitude 'on three' than they could manage themselves. Nevertheless their presence was always comforting and sometimes was vitally necessary, though several such incidents ended in total disaster.

Sqn Ldr (Retd) David Guthrie recalls the loss of a USAF B-36 in the Atlantic in August 1953. The aircraft's distress call was picked up by a civil airliner and relayed to the UK SAR authorities. David Guthrie as captain of the nominated SAR Shackleton at Aldergrove took off, but, as he later discovered, searched a sea area several hundred miles from the point where the B-36 had actually ditched and where some survivors were eventually found.

In September 1962 a Super Constellation with 57 American servicemen, seven of their wives, two children and eight crew aboard lost three out of its four engines off the southwest coast of Ireland and made a reasonably successful ditching with 50 of those aboard reaching a liferaft, many of them injured and suffering from skin burns from the petrol-polluted water. They were spotted by a Shackleton which directed the freighter *Celerina* to them. Six died in the liferaft and 17 needed urgent hospital treatment. The worst casualties were winched from the ship's deck by RAF and USAF rescue helicopters and flown to the Irish mainland, some being given preliminary treatment on board a Canadian aircraft carrier.

On a December night in 1963 the Greek-owned cruise liner *Lakonia* with many British passengers aboard caught fire about 500 miles west of Gibraltar. The now Gp Capt David Leppard, then of No 224 Squadron, scrambled in Mk 2 WL757 from the 'Rock' at first light. He and his crew found the ship burning from its bows to within about 100ft of the stern and for miles around they could see liferafts, some filled with people, some half-full, many of the occupants apparently already dead. During an 11-hour sortie they dropped both their sets of Lindholme Gear and had the satisfaction of seeing survivors climb aboard the nine-man liferaft of the first one. They then did their best to co-ordinate the many other rescue attempts by at least five ships and by a US Navy DC-6 which had diverted to the area during a transit flight from the Azores. At the end of some eight hours overhead of a very distressing scene they were able to report by radio that all living persons seen were reasonably safe in lifeboats or rafts. The final death toll in the *Lakonia* disaster was 128 out of 1,032 souls on board. It could have been higher but for the efforts of David Leppard and the crew of Shackleton WL757, callsign 'Playmate 72'.

On 5 February 1960 the 7,000-ton US freighter *Valley Forge* ran aground on a small island in the South China Sea to the north-east of Singapore. A Shackleton of No 205 Squadron from Changi, captained by Flt Lt R. Bennett, located the vessel within 15 minutes of take-off and dropped rescue gear from 90ft altitude at near stalling speed. The Second Officer of the ship later said that the equipment 'Nearly fell into our laps'. After 12 hours the crew of the stricken ship were taken off by the minesweeper HMS *Fiskerton* which had been directed to the scene by the Shackleton. One injured seaman and another with a weak heart were taken ashore quickly in a dinghy dropped by the aircraft. Both ship and aircraft crews later met up in Changi to exchange mutual congratulations in suitable circumstances.

The above examples can only be taken as a very small sample of the sort of SAR work undertaken by Shackletons during their long service.

The AEW Mark 2 aircraft operated by No 8 Squadron from Lossiemouth always carry at least one set of Lindholme Gear at all times and crews frequently train in its use. Although not 'dedicated' to the SAR role it is always recognised in the squadron that one of their aircraft on a 'barrier' AEW mission over one of the most hostile sea areas in the world could be the nearest to some sort of disaster and could react quickly to it.

Apart from this kind of SAR task Shackletons often flew on other types of 'mercy mission', one of the most dramatic of which concerned the Agadir (Morocco)

Below:
This is how the crew of WL757 saw the *Lakonia*. This picture was taken by the then Fl Off R.P.D. Milwright, the aircraft navigator. Mr Milwright is now a veterinary surgeon in Cambridgeshire.

Right:
A goodwill mission. Mk 1s flying over the sacred city of Anuradhapura in Sri Lanka (then Ceylon). *MoD*

Below right:
A Mk 2 WG554 of 42 Squadron flying over Durban in April 1953. This visit and a subsequent one by No 204 Squadron two years later were instrumental in the purchase of Mk 3s by the South African Air Force. This fairly early Mk 2 is still sporting its dorsal gun turret. *MoD*

earthquake of 1960 which killed more than 12,000 people. Among aircraft of many nations the Mk 2 Shackletons of No 244 Squadron from Gibraltar played a prominent part in the relief operations.

Agadir lay some 500 miles southwest of Gibraltar and ground and air crews of '224' worked through the night of 1/2 March to load supplies into the bomb-bay panniers, including food, tents, blankets and medical equipment. Sqn Ldr (Retd) N.G. Ashcroft recalls how 'Airway Red' from Tangier via Casablanca and into Agadir was crowded with RT traffic in different accents as relief aircraft moved in to try to help. After off-loading relief supplies the '224' crews were then asked to take survivors out – rather surprisingly, to France. Two Shackletons delivered 42 women and children to Istres, with babies being washed in the galleys and their bottles being sterilised in the tea-making machine.

Other No 224 Squadron Shackletons flew in specialist medical teams, clothing, drugs and cigarettes, and on one sad occasion 2,400lb of quicklime for the necessary communal graves. A newspaper correspondent was also lifted as a passenger on this flight.

Although their natural element was always over the sea, Shackletons did on several occasions assist those in distress on the land. One item of equipment normally held in the bomb bay is called the 'CLE', or 'Container Land Equipment', which is usually dropped by parachute and contains about 400lb of survival items. One was used 'for real' in July 1962 by a No 37 Squadron aircraft from Khormaksar (Aden) when a Beaver of the Desert Locust Survey Organisation was reported overdue up-country. The crashed aeroplane was spotted by Flg Off Burden and his crew and a CLE dropped. They also spotted a

ground rescue team approaching in Land Rovers and homed them in by dropping messages. Unfortunately they also saw what appeared to be the dead body of the Beaver pilot about 50yd from the wreckage. It later transpired that he had survived the crash but had been shot by local bandits. Such was life – and death – in the Western Aden Protectorate in the 1960s.

One of the last 'overland' rescues recorded in which a Shackleton was involved followed the crash of a civilian helicopter, carrying a film cameraman, during the 1977 blizzards in northern Scotland. The helicopter was forced down on a frozen loch and the pilot and passenger set out to walk in −5°C temperature. A full rescue alert was mounted when they were overdue, and one of their pocket miniflares was seen by an alert crewman in a No 8 Squadron Shackleton from Lossiemouth. An RAF Whirlwind rescue helicopter later picked up both men.

The finding and ultimate rescuing of downed service aircrews has for many years been facilitated by the use of 'personal locater beacons' which have been continuously improved through the various code-named variants. Shackletons were involved in the trials of one of the first of such devices, code-named 'Walter'. The development of survival dinghy wireless transmitters began as early as 1941 after the serious losses of pilots who baled out over the Channel during the Battle of Britain and after the capture of a fairly efficient device used by the Luftwaffe. The development of 'Walter', a beacon which was designed to help a searching aircraft find a survivor over the last five miles of its search pattern, began in 1943, and by the end of World War 2 was part of the standard equipment of RAF aircraft required to fly over the sea.

Numerous exercises – and some 'live' SAR operations – involving the use of 'Walter' were carried out by Shackletons in the 1950s but with only limited success. Many of the failures were attributed to the fact that the signals emitted by 'Walter' beacons were very similar to the emissions from faulty submarine telegraph and telephone cables. However, 'Walter'

Below:
A 'one-off job'. Sir Francis Chichester in *Gipsy Moth IV* being welcomed home by a St Mawgan Shackleton about 400 miles west of Plymouth. *The Times*

was improved into 'Sarah' (Search and Rescue Homing Beacon), then into 'Sarbe' (Search and Rescue Beacon), and eventually into an even more sophisticated device, with hundreds of Service airmen owing their lives to the latter three.

Nuclear Weapon Trials
Shackleton squadrons played prominent parts in several aspects of the development of nuclear weapons by Britain and other Western nations in the 1950s. In June 1956 a detachment from No 269 Squadron flew to Australia to take part in early experiments based on Darwin and Alice Springs, and two aircraft of No 206 Squadron carried out eastwards circumnavigations of the world while helping in the establishment of the Christmas Island base.

Nos 206 and 240 Squadrons were involved in the 1957 Christmas Island tests and aircraft from No 224 Squadron and from the 'Ballykelly Wing' covered the 1958 tests, with a Mk 3 of No 206 Squadron carrying out a proving flight. No 204 Squadron was also involved in further Australian tests in 1957 at the Maralinga research grounds.

The Christmas Island tests bore the code-name 'Grapple' and the Shackletons taking part carried the insignia of a red cormorant clutching at a grapple hook on their fins. Sqn Ldr (Retd) Denys Swarbrick recalls that living conditions during the 'Grapple' operation were primitive, although there was much to interest both ground and air crews. The dusty coral atoll had a maximum elevation of 15ft above sea level and all concerned lived in tents, in which particular skills with empty orange boxes were required to keep camp beds at a safe altitude above the large and perpetually active land crabs.

The main tasks for the Shackletons were meteorological observations and the warning-off of any shipping straying into the test areas. One steamer which did stray into a test area was seen by a Shackleton crew to develop a double bow-wave after they had dropped their multi-language leaflets on to its deck. A copy of Lloyd's Register held at their base stated that the ship in question was capable of a maximum 8kt.

Showing the Flag
With their ability to fly to almost any part of the world as self-contained units with ground crews, very-long-range fuel tanks in the bomb bays and stocks of spares aboard, Shackletons inherited this important role from their 'Flying Boat Union' predecessors. They carried out several world circumnavigations as well as Polar flights. These goodwill flights, many of great political significance in the international melting-pot era of the 1950s–1970s, involved journeys of up to 40,000 miles. All were carried out without serious accident although there were many 'incidents' which in particular stretched the ingenuity and improvisation skills of the travelling engineer officers and ground crews.

Weather Ship Suppliers
Shackleton crews made many firm friends in the British Meteorological Service as carriers of mail and urgently needed supplies to the Weather Ships on vigil in mid-Atlantic in the era before satellites, and they were always particularly welcome around Christmas time.

These sorties doubled up as valuable long range navigation exercises for the aircraft and as opportunities for the Weather Ships to test their own position-checking and homing equipment. For the Shackletons they usually involved 16 to 18-hour round trips with considerable pride being taken in the precision of the final drop – the objective being to put the packages within boat hook reach of the ship's bows or at least within a few oar strokes or propeller turns of one of its boats.

Below:
A little bit of showing off and proving that not only fighters can fly in close formation. Mk 2s of No 224 Squadron. *courtesy John Latimer*

5
The South African Shackletons

In the early 1950s the South African Air Force began to seek replacements for its fleet of Sunderlands which still maintained 'the watch' over the Cape of Good Hope shipping lanes and carried out many other maritime reconnaissance tasks including search and rescue. The Sunderlands were operated by No 35 Squadron SAAF which had been formed at the end of World War 2, out of No 262 Squadron RAF which had been based in South Africa from 1942, operating Catalinas from Congella, Durban, with detachments at St Lucia on the northern natal coast and at Langebaan, north of Capetown. The posting of SAAF personnel into No 262 Squadron began in late 1943 and the first SAAF Commanding Officer, Maj R.D. Madeley, took over in July 1944. The unit was restyled

No 35 Squadron SAAF on 2 February 1945 with 12 Catalinas on strength and 462 personnel.

The first three of an eventual 16 Sunderland GR Mk 5s were delivered in April 1945, flying first with RAF serial numbers but later with the 1701-plus numbers allocated to South African maritime reconnaissance aircraft. Between November 1945 and February 1946 the No 35 Squadron Sunderlands were mainly used to repatriate South African servicemen from the Mediterranean theatre of war in rather the same manner as the RAF Lancasters were used in Operation 'Dodge'.

The Sunderlands served faithfully until 1957 but before then the South African Government had been impressed by two goodwill visits of RAF Shackleton

Left:
The first Shackleton to be delivered to the SAAF, No 1716, on finals to runway 19 at D.F. Malan Airport. Table Mountain and 'Lion's Head' are in the background. This aircraft, pictured in 1977, was still in service in 1984. *L.J. Vosloo*

Above:
A formation off Table Mountain. *L.J. Vosloo*

Below:
The front end of SAAF Shackleton No 1719. *L.J. Vosloo*

squadrons and had become especially interested in the development plans for a Mk 3 version of this aircraft. An order was placed with A.V. Roe's for eight Mk 3 Shackletons, initially in the Phase 1 form, later to be up-graded to Phase 2, and eventually to Phase 3, but for a number of reasons the Viper jets were never fitted to the South African aircraft as they were to the RAF's Mk 3 Phase 3s.

One of the reasons for the absence of the Vipers was that the 6,000ft runway requirement of the RAF did not apply in South Africa. In the event the decision was a beneficial one for the SAAF since its Mk 3s long outlived those of the RAF, with less strain being imposed on the airframes. The SAAF claims that it put its first Mk 3 Shackleton into operational service slightly ahead of the RAF – by 12 days in fact – and it certainly kept its last one flying for many years after the latter Service, indeed until the time of writing this book in late-1984.

In February 1957 when, of course, relations between the UK and South Africa were still cordial, a party of 41 officers, NCOs and men of No 35 Squadron travelled to the Avro airfield at Woodford for an intensive familiarisation course on the aircraft. Led by the Squadron CO, Commandant M.J. Uys, the party also trained at RAF St Mawgan, taking part in joint exercises in some of their own aircraft during the summer of 1957.

The first two SAAF Shackletons, Nos 1716 and 1717, were officially handed over at Woodford on 21 May 1957. During the changeover from Sunderlands to Shackletons No 35 Squadron moved its headquarters from the Congella flying boat base at

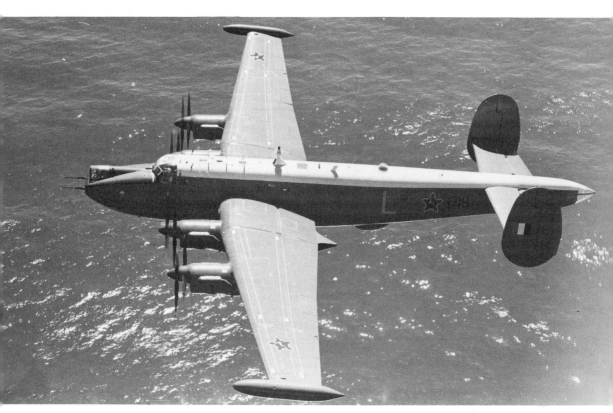

Durban to Capetown. Here the existing SAAF airfield at Ysterplaat was inadequate for aircraft of this size so a section of the D.F. Malan civil airport was allocated to house the Shackletons with Ysterplaat retained as a maintenance and administration facility. Early Shackleton operations and exercises were also carried out from Waterkloof, Pretoria.

The first operational exercises carried out by the South African Shackletons were styled 'border patrols', involving flights of up to 3,000 miles and 15 hours, mainly along the northern border to 'show the flag' and possibly check on violations. Although enjoyable for the aircrews who could watch the passage of their spectacular national landscape from tree-top level, these missions were not considered to be cost-effective, most of the reports submitted concerning the scattering of herds of elephant and antelope in face of the four-Griffon growl. They were discarded in favour of patrols along the west coast where an intensification of Soviet shipping movements was observed at the turn of the 1950s/1960s.

The South African Shackletons have frequently been involved in SAR missions. Initially three of their aircraft were fitted with Saunders-Roe airborne lifeboats, but, as in the RAF, they were discarded in favour of Lindholme Gear at a fairly early stage.

Probably the most dramatic South African Shackleton SAR mission occurred in 1965 when one of eight Mk 50 Buccaneers on a delivery flight from the

Left:
No 1719 which was finally withdrawn from service in 1978. *L.J. Vosloo*

Below left:
The badge of No 35 Squadron SAAF.

Below:
As in the RAF, airborne lifeboats were installed in SAAF Shackletons but soon abandoned in favour of Lindholme Gear. This SARO Mk 3 boat is now on display at the SAAF Museum in Pretoria. *L.J. Vosloo*

Bottom:
No 1721 of the SAAF at D.F. Malan Airport. This aircraft with the least remaining fatigue hours remained in operational service until November 1984. *L.J. Vosloo*

UK lost both engines at high altitude over the South Atlantic, to the north of the later world-famous Ascension Island, with both crew members ejecting. The problem and the ejection was observed and reported by the Buccaneer formation leader (Maj A.M. Muller), and SAAF Shackleton No 1722, located on stand-by at Bissau and captained by Maj Pat Conway, took off and soon picked up blips from two 'Sarah' personal locater beacons. On closing in, green and red flares were exchanged as per the Search, Rescue and Survival handbook. A second SAAF Shackleton based at Bissau (No 1721) captained by Major Chris Lombard joined in the rescue operation. Flares and two sets of Lindholme Gear were dropped and eventually the two crewmen of the Buccaneer,

Capts Jooste and de Kerk, were picked up by the ship *Randfontein* which was guided to the scene by Shackleton No 1722. The two officers were still reasonably comfortable in the MS 9 liferaft from the Lindholme Gear dropped to them.

The total time flown by Maj Conway's Shackleton 1722 was 18 hours. Two SAAF Hercules aircraft (Nos 403 and 405) also assisted in what has been recorded as a classic air-sea rescue operation with all the advance preparations, all the drills, and all the equipment working according to plan.

As recorded in detail later the distinguished service of the Shackletons in South Africa was marred by the accident which killed all 13 crew members of No 1718 on 8 August 1963. The South African Mk 3s were also inevitably involved in a number of lesser accidents, several involving failure of the then recently-built tricycle undercarriage during heavyish landings.

Indeed, upon landing in full view of the South Africa press at the end of its delivery flight in 1958, No 1723 suffered hydraulic failure and in order to avoid over-running the runway on to a busy main road the pilot decided to swing the aircraft into a brick building, which badly bent his No 1 engine and its nacelle.

Another landing, by No 1720 at D.F. Malan airport in September 1961, received prominent media coverage. In one of those human errors with which RAF Shackleton crews were well acquainted two engines on the same side were shut down during a practice asymmetric approach, resulting in an

Below:
No 1717 of the SAAF. This aircraft was kept flying until March 1984 with 5,999 hours on its airframe, partly because of the successful cannibalisation of the remains of No 1718 after the latter's crash in the Steynskloof mountains in 1963. *L.J. Vosloo*

undershoot, the loss of most of the undercarriage and the best part of two engines. Both these aircraft were repaired locally and the accidents put down to experience without many hard feelings.

The potential of the Shackleton 'in anger' was well demonstrated in South Africa in 1971 when the 70,000-ton oil tanker *Wafra* ran aground off Cape Agulhas, threatening to spill its cargo of 60,000 tons of crude oil on to cherished beaches and nature reserves. A tug pulled the ship off the rocks and towed it into open water 200 miles south of the Cape, and the SAAF was then required to sink it, preferably in one piece without rupturing the oil cargo tanks.

Buccaneer S-50s from No 24 Squadron SAAF first did their best using Nord AS-30 air-to-surface missiles, but failed after two attempts, the whole affair being remarkably similar to that involving the tanker *Torrey Canyon* off the coast of Cornwall. The Shackletons of

No 35 Squadron were around all the time, initially to observe, record, and co-ordinate the Buccaneer strikes. Eventually two No 3 Squadron Shackletons dropped a number of Mk II depth charges alongside the *Wafra* and sank her without trace, perhaps proving (as a cartoonist of No 8 Squadron RAF later said in one of his captions): 'Eight Screws are better than Two Blow-jobs'.

In a more serious vein the main roles for the surviving seven of the SAAF Mk 3 Shackletons (progressively up-dated to Phase 3 but always without the Viper jets) over a period of 27 years have been concerned with a continuous watch over the Cape of Good Hope shipping routes. Their tasks have included fishery protection patrols and, of course, other search and rescue operations over the vast sea areas of the Atlantic and Indian Oceans within their 'manor'. It is estimated that more than 2,000 ships pass the Cape

every month, among them about 30 oil tankers every day. Sightings by SAAF Shackletons since 1968 – when it was first detected that Russian warships were entering the Indian Ocean – are claimed by South African sources to have included the helicopter-carrier *Leningrad,* at least two 'Kara' class guided missile destroyers and the 'Kiev' class carrier *Novorossiysk* to name but a few, with obviously many more to be added to the list by the time this book appears.

Another important task which has fallen to the Shackletons of No 35 Squadron SAAF has been the provision of top cover to civil aircraft of South African Airways and other airlines plying over the Indian Ocean en route to destinations in Australia and elsewhere.

Left:
Things went wrong of course. SAAF Shackleton No 1721 after a belly landing at Ysterplaat on 10 September 1962. In this picture rocket rails can be seen underneath the port wing. This form of equipment was ordered and installed by the SAAF. The Royal Air Force at one stage 'toyed' with the idea but abandoned it. *L.J. Vosloo*

Below left:
No 1722, still flying with about 90 hours airframe fatigue life left in 1984. *L.J. Vosloo*

Below:
Nosewheel assemblies sometimes caused problems for both RAF and SAAF users. This is No 1722 at Langebaanweg SAAF base in July 1960. The rocket rails are again visible under the port wing. *L.J. Vosloo*

In August 1975 a Shackleton crew was briefed that Portuguese refugees from the civil war in Angola were making their way south to Walvis Bay in small boats. On 24 August Capt Van Dyk and crew took off in No 1720, and after initially obtaining no sightings at sea turned inland and spotted about 200 refugees scattered around the Cunene River mouth having travelled south by road. Later they sighted a total of about 40 small and perilously overloaded vessels at sea and reported details to their Maritime Command. On return they saw the word 'Bread' scrawled on the desert sand near the Cunene River mouth. On that and the following day they dropped food containers and kept track of the refugee vessels, one of which sank. It was believed that without the SAAF intervention – made without any official request – many of the refugees would have died in the Namib Desert.

Although details remain classified it is known that Shackletons flew some 200 hours on operational sorties during the Angolan Civil War.

On 23 November 1984 the SAAF Shackletons were finlly withdrawn from service with the last Mk 3s airborne anywhere in the world carrying out a line-abreast formation fly-past over Capetown. They were Nos 1716, 1721 and 1722, all destined to be placed as memorials to the type as airfield gate guards or in museums. Airframe hours for the SAAF Shackletons had ranged between 4,500 and 7,000. One aircraft, No 1717, was kept flying after a technical team had ascended into the Steynskloof mountains to

ARMS EMBARGO PREVENTS THE REPLACEMENT OF SHACKLETONS..

cannibalise the wreckage of No 1718 which had crashed there many years earlier.

In efforts to conserve the SAAF Shackletons' fatigue life medium-range search and rescue tasks were earlier allocated to No 27 Squadron equipped with Piaggio 166S Albatrosses, and in 1984 a contract was being contemplated with SAFAIR, a commercial air freight company, to take over long distance SAR responsibilities with Lockheed L-100-30s.

This is a book about an aeroplane and is not concerned in any way with international or national politics but it should record the fact that in 1984/85 the South African Government was 'shopping' for suitable replacements for its then moribund Shackletons. It was fairly widely known in 1984 that this was a subject raised in talks between the South African Prime Minister Mr Botha and Mrs Thatcher and that the SAAF had expressed a special desire for the purchase of British Aerospace Coastguarders – versions of the well-proven 748 design. The request to purchase a fleet of these seemingly innocuous aircraft was refused by HM Government on the grounds that such an arrangement would transgress the United Nations arms embargo.

When first ordered the SAAF Shackletons were painted in 'Extra Dark Sea Grey' on upper surfaces, 'PRU Blue' on fuselage sides and wing and tailplane undersides, and with yellow or black serial numbers. The first three aircraft were delivered with blue and white roundels with a Springbok superimposed – the

Above:
The issue of obtaining replacements for the SAAF Shackletons in 1984 because of the UN arms embargo drew down this cartoon in *The Cape Argus*.

traditional markings of SAAF aircraft for many years. The insignia were changed during the delivery period with all the aircraft eventually bearing the current 'Castle' national markings. Soon after delivery fuselage roofs were painted white to reduce cabin heat, and red propeller spinners were introduced in the early 1970s.

The first SAAF Shackleton to be grounded on fatigue hour figures was No 1723 on 22 November 1977, followed by No 1719 on 24 April 1978 and by 1720 on 10 March 1983. The last-numbered aircraft was set up as a gate guard at Air Force Base Ysterplaat on 28 October 1983.

Other temporary expedients to fill the gap left by the grounding of the SAAF Shackletons included the increased use of their C-130 Hercules aircraft in the reconnaissance role as well as the medium-range Albatrosses, and the conversion of the SAS *Tafelberg*, a fleet replenishment auxiliary, into a helicopter carrier for offshore SAR work.

In late 1984 it was announced that No 35 Squadron SAAF would have its Shackletons temporarily replaced by maritime reconnoissance version Dakotas – thus proving something about the value of age and experience.

6
Crashes and Losses

The total tally of Shackleton losses includes 14 catastrophic and fatal crashes involving 141 deaths. One 'incident' involved the loss of two aircraft on the same night, and a mid-air collision between them was recorded as 'the least improbable' cause. The totals include the loss of the Mk 3 prototype WR970 on 7 December 1956, described in some detail in Chapter 2, and of the South African Air Force Mk 3 on 8 August 1963.

After four fatal accidents in the six months between November 1967 and April 1968, Mr Merlyn Rees, then Under-Secretary for Defence (RAF), answered a private notice question in the Commons on the type's safety record, particularly in view of its by then already long service. He stated that there was no evidence to show fatigue as a common cause of the recent spate of accidents, indeed that there was no evidence of any single common factor. The aircraft involved, he said, had flown respectively 5,971, 3,620, 3,814 and 2,525 hours, relatively low figures compared with the total fatigue life of the design, and all had had major refits. There was no evidence that the age of the aircraft had contributed to any of the accidents and no valid reason for grounding Shackletons.

The details of the catastrophic accidents below show only two possibly prevalent causes – engine overspeeding perhaps attributable to the complicated 'translation unit' between the hubs of the contra-rotating propellers, and the sheer operational necessity of carrying out quite violent low level manoeuvres in a very heavy aircraft.

The fatal accidents were:

25 June 1952: Mk 1 VP261 of No 120 Squadron with some No 240 Squadron personnel on board. Twelve killed, one survivor.

This Aldergrove-based aircraft was taking part in an anti-submarine exercise in the North Sea. After dropping two smoke bombs on a submarine it was seen to turn, level off to start a second run and then crash into the sea.

A stall in the final turn or loss of power due to the master fuel cocks being knocked off were advanced as possible causes. The latter possibility resulted in a general warning to crews and to the fitting of a cover over the fuel cocks to nullify the risk of an unharnessed crewman falling across them during low level manoeuvres.

8 October 1952: Mk 1 VP286 of 236 OCU. Fourteen killed, no survivors.

The aircraft was on an air-to-sea gunnery exercise in the Moray Firth in daylight. Nothing was heard from it to indicate trouble but at 13.44hrs observers at a considerable distance saw a bright flash and black smoke in the Tarbat Ness area. A stall during the type of steep turn employed on such exercises was suspected as the cause and pilots were warned of the necessity to apply adequate power during such manoeuvres.

11 December 1953: Mk 2 WL746 of No 240 Squadron. Ten killed, no survivors.

The aircraft, from Ballykelly, was on an anti-submarine and navigation exercise off the Argyllshire coast. It reported its submarine exercise completed at 17.15hrs and promised a further call at 17.45. The second call was not made and a witness on land reported hearing an aircraft very low overhead, its engines stopping and an explosion. Wreckage was found in the sea indicating 'a very violent impact'. No cause was advanced.

12 February 1954: Mk 2 WL794 of No 38 Squadron. Ten killed, no survivors. The aircraft took off from Luqa (Malta) at 02.16hrs and reported it was carrying out a radar approach on to a submarine to be followed by a practice attack. A flash and a glow on the surface of the sea were seen from a ship. No cause was advanced.

11 January 1955: Mk 2s WG531 and WL743 of No 42 Squadron. Eighteen killed, no survivors.

In this, the most catastrophic of all the Shackleton accidents, the two aircraft left St Eval at 10.14 and 10.20hrs respectively to carry a 15-hour patrol and search exercise to the south of the Fastnet Rock off Southern Ireland.

The first aircraft off, captained by Flg Off George Board, was 14 minutes late due to reasons beyond his control and the second (Pilot Officer Wood) left early, thus reducing the normal half-hour separation time to six minutes. This factor tended to lend credence to the inevitable theory that the two aircraft were lost in a collision, possibly following each other in a 'creeping line ahead' search pattern or by practising homing on to one another.

The CO of 42 Squadron at the time, Sqn Ldr Norman Wilson, now living in retirement in Southport, has however never been entirely convinced by the collision theory finally recorded as 'the least improbable', particularly as radio messages were received indicating that the two captains had adjusted their separation and that up to 20.00 hrs that night were flying at the prescribed 85 miles distance from one another.

In the event all contact was lost from 20.58hrs when a ground radio operator attempted to call PO Wood with a barometric pressure reading over his exercise area which he had requested earlier. There was no reply from him and neither aircraft made their scheduled 21.00 nor 22.00hrs reports. In spite of an enormous search operation involving other Shackletons, Lancasters, Sunderlands and many smaller aircraft as well as surface ships no trace was found of either aircraft until more than 11 years later when the starboard outer engine of PO Wood's aircraft was trawled up off the southwest Irish coast, about 75 miles north of the assumed collision point.

7 December 1956: Mk 3 Prototype WR970 on test by A.V. Roe Ltd from Woodford. Four killed, no survivors (see Chapter 2).

10 January 1958: T-4 VP259 of the Maritime Operational Training Unit. Two killed, four injured.

This Kinloss-based aircraft was carrying out roller landing practice and hit trees on 800ft high ground near Elgin. The dead were the two pilots. No cause was declared.

9 December 1958: Mk 1 VP254 of No 205 Squadron. Eleven killed, no survivors.

The aircraft, code letter 'B', took off from Labuan Island, Northern Borneo, at 05.48hrs local time on a routine anti-piracy patrol. Its Captain was Flt Lt W.A.S. Boutell and in addition to his normal crew of nine he had aboard Mr A.R. Miller, the Acting Deputy Police Commissioner of Northern Borneo.

Shortly after departure the aircraft was diverted to investigate a report of shipwrecked fishermen stranded on an atoll 280 miles north of Labuan. At 07.10hrs Flt Lt Boutell reported he had located survivors and had directed a junk to their assistance. At 11.43hrs a further report from him said the rescue operation was going smoothly and that in 15 minutes he would return to his original task. After a brief position report at 11.59hrs nothing further was heard from VP254.

An extensive air and sea search was mounted but nothing was found until the sixth day when Flt Lt John Elias and his crew in another '205' Shackleton spotted the markings 'B 205' laid out in white coral rock on a sandy beach on Sin Cowe island at 09.53N/114.20E. On 16 December the Royal New Zealand Navy frigate *Rotoiti* put a landing party on the island and found a grave marked with a wooden cross on which 'B 205' had been carved. They also found an RAF officer's cap

Above left:
Wreathes being loaded preparatory to dropping over the sea area where WG531 and WL743 were presumed to have crashed. *Sqn Ldr Norman Wilson*

Above:
Shackleton 'H' of No 42 Squadron about to take off with the wreathes aboard. *Sqn Ldr Norman Wilson*

and an aircrew watch. The body in the grave was first transferred to the aircraft carrier HMS *Albion* whose helicopters later removed the simple cross. At Labuan the body was identified as that of Flt Sgt D.N.G. Dancy, the flight engineer of VP254.

Eventually officers from HMS *Albion* traced a Chinese fisherman, Gan Chung-Huang, Captain of the *Ray Fu Chen*, who with his crew had seen VP254 crash into the sea soon after passing low over them about seven miles south of Sin Cowe island. All that the fishermen had found were Flt Sgt Dancy's body, the cap and the watch, and remembering the markings they had seen on the side of the Shackleton, they had taken the body to the island, buried it reverently and in the Christian manner, and carved out the little wooden cross with 'B 205'. Guessing that a search would be made they also laid out the markings on the beach.

Flt Sgt Dancy's body was taken to Singapore and re-interred in the Military Cemetery there on 19 December 1958, the service attended by the Commander-in-Chief Far East Air Force, Air Marshal the Earl of Bandon, other senior RAF officers and

representatives of all ranks from No 205 Squadron. The cross was re-erected beside St George's Chapel at RAF Changi where it stood until 19 August 1971, when during the British withdrawal from the Far East it was flown to the UK in the last Shackleton of No 205 Squadron to leave. It was finally placed in the parish church of St Eval, Cornwall, in many senses a 'home' for '205' and for all the Shackletons. A brass plaque alongside records the names of all the crew of VP254 and a framed document records the story outlined above. Captain Gan Chung-Huang later received a letter of thanks and cash award for himself and his crew for their efforts from HM Consul at Tamsui, Taiwan.

No definite cause of the crash was recorded but the possibility of loss of orientation or misjudgment of height at low level over a glassy-calm sea was considered as the most likely one.

8 August 1953: Mk 3 No 1718 of No 35 Squadron South African Air Force. Thirteen killed, no survivors.

This aircraft was taking part in a joint British/South African CAPEX exercise and was in transit between Capetown and Port Elizabeth when it struck high ground in the Steynskloof mountains near Worcester.

Although the cause was never positively established weather conditions in the area at the time included winds gusting to 80kt and icing conditions down to 3,000ft. The speculation was that the aircraft may have been blown off course – it was taking a 'short cut' at the time to keep up with the exercise – and also encountered severe icing problems. It took several days for ground rescuers to reach the scene and establish that there had been no survivors.

8 December 1965: Mk 3 XF704 of No 201 Squadron. Eight killed, three survivors.

During a transit flight between Gan, the RAF staging post in the Indian Ocean, and Changi, Singapore, this aircraft's No 4 engine caught fire following overspeeding. The fire spread to the starboard wing, which folded. Nevertheless the captain and co-pilot (both of whom were among the dead) appeared to be able to keep the aircraft almost level until final impact with the result that two signallers and a passenger survived and were rescued 11 hours later by HMS *Ajax*.

19 November 1967: Mk 3 WR976 of No 201 Squadron. Nine killed, two survivors.

This aircraft, based at Kinloss but detached to St Mawgan, was taking part in an anti-submarine exercise 200 miles off the Cornish coast and was seen to hit the sea in a descending turn while carrying out a mock attack. No specific reason was recorded.

21 December 1967: Mk 3 XF702 of No 206 Squadron. Eleven killed, no survivors.

The aircraft, flying on a routine training mission, hit the ground at Creag Bhan, Lochailort, Inverness-shire

in extreme weather conditions. Turbulence and icing were advanced as possible causes.

19 April 1968: Mk 2 WB833 (a former Mk 2 prototype) of No 210 Squadron. Eleven killed, no survivors.

This Ballykelly-based aircraft was exercising with HM Submarine *Onyx* in the Clyde Estuary and hit 400ft high ground on the Mull of Kintyre. A small navigational error putting the aircraft over land instead of sea was recorded as the likely cause.

Two other unfortunate fatal accidents involved a crewman falling through an escape hatch and an engineering officer being run over on the ground.

Several other Shackletons were of course written off in non-fatal accidents, one of the most curious entries in the 'Struck off Charge' list being perhaps the fate of WR986 of No 204 Squadron in September 1971, the cause recorded being 'Rodent Damage'.

The first write-off loss listed was in Gibraltar in August 1951 when VP283 of No 224 Squadron hit the ground short of the runway and shed its main landing

Below:
The wreathes are dropped.   *Sqn Ldr Norman Wilson*

Right:
Mk 3 prototype WR970, which crashed in Derbyshire on stall tests in December 1956.   *British Aerospace*

wheels. A belly landing was made without too much physical pain on a nearby beach but perhaps understandably little detail was put on permanent record. Mr Jimmy Orrell of Avro recalls being despatched to Gibraltar to give some general advice on handling techniques at low level with an aeroplane which was operating at an early stage of its career from a runway which has never been exactly popular with the pilots of 'heavies'.

One Shackleton was destroyed and three others damaged by fire at A.V. Roe's subsidiary factory at Langar, Nottinghamshire in December 1955, the burnt-out aircraft unfortunately being fitted with special test equipment and due to fly to Malta on the following day.

Two non-fatal write-offs deserve permanent record as tributes both to the ruggedness of the aircraft and to the skills of their crews in dealing with potential disaster. On 10 January 1964 the then Flt Lt John ('Pop') Gladstone AFC of No 120 Squadron took Mk 3 XF710 off from Kinloss for a night exercise and almost immediately encountered overspeeding of up to 3,300rpm in his No 3 engine which then caught fire and fell off into the sea. A few seconds later his flight engineer reported that the fire warning light was showing on No 4 and they had to feather it. Breaking thin cloud and seeing the lights of Inverness ahead and only 1,000ft below them, Flt Lt Gladstone and his co-pilot Flg Off J.A.W. Lee managed to skid the aircraft clear of the city while it was still shedding burning wreckage in spite of their having little, if any, lateral control. By the light of the flames from his own aircraft Flt Lt Gladstone then selected a reasonably level and tree-less stretch of Culloden Moor which was clear of, though fairly close to, the village of Smithton. The aircraft first bounced about 75ft and finally came to rest some 350ft from the original impact point. As the citation for the well-deserved second Bar to his AFC recorded, Flt Lt Gladstone immediately organised the safe evacuation of his crew, five of whom were slightly injured and the remainder unscathed – at least physically. Before leaving the scene he directed the operations of the local fire brigade, in particular advising them where pyrotechnics, explosives and fuel were located. Very soon afterwards the crew were being comforted by the inhabitants of Smithton, most of whom were attending a barn dance at the time.

Twenty years later Sqn Ldr (Retd) John Gladstone wrote to the author:

'My memories of the occasion are of a lovely black, clear winter night with a slight layer of cloud at four thousand feet. A feeling of well-being and satisfaction at having got airborne after earlier delays, a swing on the rudder that indicated an engine failure, a massive over-confidence in my ability to handle an engine failure after so many drills and the odd previous failures, punctured by a shout from the engineer "Christ, it's on fire".

Above:
The 'B 205' Cross in St Eval Parish Church. *Air Historical Branch*

Above right:
Firemen from Inverness Fire Brigade and from RAF Kinloss moving in to the tail section of XF710. The local (Inverness) Fire Brigade was not equipped with foam and this had to be brought from Kinloss.

Right:
The remains of a miracle. XF710 lying on Culloden Moor, her entire aircrew having escaped. Evidence can be seen of where the first fire started in No 3 engine and the remains of No 4 engine on what is left of the starboard wing. Sonobuoys and the rear starboard door can be detected on the ground to the right side of the picture.

'How can anyone describe the moment of panic following a cry like that and the sadness gripping your throat because maybe you won't see your wife and kids again?

'Fortunately the training and the drills take over and you get stuck into sorting it out. Not very well perhaps, it's all a tangle of huffing and puffing and trying to keep the wings level now.

'Then you can see the trees – the burning wing made a gorgeous landing light – you heave back on the stick and bang, thud, wallop, you've arrived and in one piece more or less.

'Good old Shack, built like a battleship.

'A mad scramble to get out, a quick check on heads and we're all sitting in the back room of the local

barndance among ladies dispensing hot tea. And lovely polite Scots fellows sidle in with bottles to the disapproving stares of the ladies.

'And a farmer appears, dishevelled. "By God" he says, "I was just taking off my breeks when I saw this flaming apparition through the window. I didna know whether to drop my breeks and pray or pull them up and run." '

One of XF710's signallers, Sgt James Hamilton, completed the log, entering the words 'Fell at Culloden' in the 'termination of flight' section. (Sgt Hamilton was later killed in a Vulcan accident).

On 14 September 1957 No 224 Squadron's Mk 2 WL792 was due to fly past in a Battle of Britain anniversary display at Gibraltar – this was a period when such performances by Shackletons often included a demonstration of their ability to fly with one, even two, engines feathered. Some four miles out and at only 500ft No 3 engine oversped. The aircraft captain began the feathering action himself and because of noise created by the screaming engine could not communicate with the rest of his crew. His well-meaning co-pilot identified No 4 as the culprit engine and feathered that, resulting in a snap decision and a spectacular wheels-up landing in front of the crowd, some of whom are believed to have thought it was all part of the show. A small fire in the bomb bay resulted from the impact but was put out by the aircrew who were all uninjured. The undamaged tail section of WL792 was at a later stage added to the front half of WL796 which had been damaged in Aden.

7

The 'Interim Solution' or 'Temporary Expedient' which lasted 13 years

The phrase 'Airborne Early Warning' could be used to describe the main functions of the very first military and naval flying machines – the balloons and man-lifting kites which enabled military commanders to see over high ground still in enemy hands, and their naval counterparts to see further over the horizon than the lookouts in topmasts. In the present-day context however, the phrase 'Airborne Early Warning' is really used to refer to aircraft carrying radar equipment capable of detecting in-coming aircraft or missiles flying below the horizon of ground or ship-based radar.

The need for this form of equipment was dramatically and painfully demonstrated to the US Government and to the rest of the world at Pearl Harbor. By the end of World War 2 the US Navy was employing carrier-based Grumman TBM-3W Avengers in the AEW role but they were not worked up in time to have much effect against the kamikazes and other fleet attackers before the war ended. The airborne radar used in the closing stages of World War 2 was the remarkable AN/APS 20, still in effective service to this day in an improved form, and developed hastily in the States under the project code-name of 'Cadillac'.

In Britain the Royal Navy first employed Douglas AD-4 Skyraiders, supplied under the Mutual Defence Assistance Programme from 1952, and then adopted the much-loved, portly Fairey Gannet Mk 3s as mounts for the apparently immortal AN/APS 20 radar sets in the AEW role. Forty-four Gannet AEW Mk 3s, with their double Mamba turboprops driving contra-

Left:
A Grumman Avenger as used in the AEW role. *Grumman History Center*

Above:
Fairey Gannet AEW Mk 3 – 'the insect' – with wings folded at Lossiemouth. *J.D. Ferguson*

rotating propellers and with a wing-folding system reminiscent of an insect, were built. They went into service at the end of 1960 and the last of them remained operational until after HMS *Ark Royal* entered Devonport for the last time in November 1978. The political decision to phase out conventional fixed-wing aircraft carriers from the Royal Navy aroused much controversy, but most of it was concerned with the loss of the strike and reconaissance potential provided by the Phantoms and Buccaneers, few members of the general public appreciating the loss of the airborne early warning facility provided by the ships' Gannets.

With its hopes confidently set on the early provision of modern land-based AEW aircraft, the Royal Air Force undertook to provide this form of cover for the Fleet. It was certainly not anticipated at that stage that it would be well into the late 1980s before a custom-built aircraft would be available, and the conversion of some surplus Mk 2 Maritime Reconnaissance Shackletons into the AEW role seemed an entirely logical 'interim solution'. Several such aircraft, with many years of fatigue life in their airframes, were available in the late 1960s/early 1970s because the re-equipment of No 18 Group with Nimrods was well under way. There were also plenty of AN/APS 20 radars from the Gannets previously embarked in HMS *Victorious* and *Eagle* which were de-commissioned before HMS *Ark Royal,* and from HMS *Hermes'* Gannet squadron.

Out of all that No 8 Squadron RAF was re-born on 1 January 1972: it was a former fighter unit with a distinguished history going back to World War 1. This meant an extension of operational life for at first 12 Shackletons, but the initial strength of No 8 Squadron's 12 AEW Mk 2 Shackletons was cut to six in 1981 by the then Defence Secretary, Mr John Nott – resulting in the production of a somewhat impolite sticker saying: 'Join Shackair and get Notted'. In its early days the Squadron also had two Shackleton pilot trainers on strength.

No 8 Squadron was given Lossiemouth on the Moray Firth in northeast Scotland as its home from the outset, but it had to fly initially from nearby Kinloss;

the runways at 'Lossie', formerly a Royal Naval Air Station, needing lengthening and strengthening.

Although the first visualised AEW task for the RAF had been support of the Fleet at sea, this in fact soon had to take second place to the provision of such cover within the United Kingdom Air Defence Region. The Navy eventually regained its own AEW cover to some extent by the hasty conversion of some Sea King helicopters during the Falklands War after the 'gap' was tragically demonstrated. The AEW Sea Kings were produced in record time but still only arrived in the South Atlantic when hostilities were over.

By the early 1960s a revolution was already under way in AEW techniques with the development of longer-range, more sensitive radar equipment, needing bigger and better aircraft to carry it, and with the Grumman E-2A 'Hawkeye' with its 'sock-darner mushroom' on top of its fuselage first flying in October 1960. The now historic Hawkeye basic design has been improved and developed under various numerical and code names down the years, as has been its near contemporary, the larger, always land-based, Boeing E-3 (AWACS or 'Sentry') designed around the familiar 707 airframe.

In Britain various options were studied from the late 1950s onwards for an indigenous AEW aircraft, including the possibility of a carrier-portable one based on the Hawker-Siddeley 125 businessman's jet, of a special version of the omnifarious HS 748 (Andover), and almost inevitably several ideas built around the Comet airframe. In the 1970s the NATO defence ministers were also seeking their own standard AEW aircraft and after much vacillation settled on the Boeing E-3, by then already in USAF service. As NATO vacillated the British Government decided to go it alone with the AEW Nimrod (Comet) project which had already reached an advanced design stage and was estimated to be costing about £1million a month by 1977 at that year's prices.

The length of the 'interim solution' or 'temporary expedient', which in some quarters has become something of a joke, has been brought about partly by political factors, partly by technical ones. The delay in bringing the Nimrod AEW Mk 3 into service – extending to some six years after the first predicted date – drew down much criticism and parliamentary debate in 1984 and 1985. While there were never any serious problems about the proven Comet/Nimrod

airframe design, even though in the Mk 3 it had had to be stretched considerably both fore and aft, it became clear in 1985 that Marconi had run into serious problems perfecting the complete 'Mission System Avionics' package to go inside it. At least one fully fitted Mk 3 was flying happily at the turn of 1984/85 from the new RAF AEW base at Waddington, but the RAF had not actually 'signed for it'. The whole development programme, estimated to have cost more than £1billion, had become a very hot political potato indeed.

The delay presented even more challenges and problems to those left with the responsibility of keeping the AEW Mk 2 Shackletons flying from Lossiemouth as some sort of token of the UK's ability to provide airborne early warning cover.

Operating anachronistic aircraft in the airborne early warning role in the middle 1980s seemed at first sight to be a mundane way of life, compared with the other excitements of RAF service. Nevertheless visitors to No 8 Squadron at Lossiemouth always sensed a special esprit de corps derived perhaps out of a perverse pleasure in keeping 'the Lovely Old Beasts' flying so well alongside the fast jets; perhaps out of the

necessarily self-contained structure of the squadron; and also out of the operational importance of the tasks undertaken. Young officers, NCOs and airmen still joining in late 1984 felt they were not only going to be able to claim membership of an exclusive 'last-of-the-many' club but that they would probably also quickly enter a new branch handling the first of the Nimrod Mk 3s.

By early 1985 however, with another two-year delay being forecast, it was by no means easy for the Squadron CO (Wg Cdr Malcolm Cooper) to maintain this high state of morale, particularly because of the uncertainties about domestic arrangements for those who had been posted to him on the expectation of quite short tours.

The three components of the airborne early warning task have been defined as: 'Seek, Find and Direct' – the last word, in comparison with 'Destroy', meaning that others have to complete the final task of thwarting an enemy bent upon attacking our shores or ships. So far as No 8 Squadron's Shackletons are concerned the 'Seeking and Finding' elements of the task usually begin, both in training and 'for real', with the flying of barrier patrols of pre-determined lengths and at heights decided to some extent by weather conditions. For fairly obvious reasons the 'barriers' are usually set over the Faroes Gap between Iceland and the north of Scotland and over the North Sea.

Above:
Grumman E-2A 'Hawkeye'. *Grumman History Center*

Above right:
Boeing E-3A AWACS (Airborne Warning and Control System) or 'Sentry'. *US Air Force*

Right:
'The Interim Solution' or 'The Lovely Old Beast'. Mk 2 AEW Shackleton of No 8 Squadron RAF. *RAF Lossiemouth*

Because it would obviously be absurd to expect a total force of six elderly aircraft (with four 'on the line') a good serviceability average by anyone's standards) to maintain a round-the-clock, 365-days-a-year watch, considerable reliance is placed upon a QRA (Quick Reaction Alert) system to cope with the estimated five Soviet incursions per week into UK air space.

A two-hour 'scramble' time is set on Shackleton QRAs and is usually met with many minutes in hand, although not without considerable strain on air and ground crews and their families in terms of meeting the necessary stand-by duty commitments. In its wisdom HM Government has not sanctioned the necessary expenditure for stand-by QRA crews to be equipped with bleepers, meaning that they must always be in hearing range of telephones throughout their very frequent duty periods.

The QRA system was evolved when No 8

No 8 Squadron Shackleton AEW2s

Top left:
Close-up of the AEW radome. *Peter R. March*

Above left:
A Shacketon shows its age. *Peter R. March*

Left :
WR963, fondly nick-named 'Parsley'. *Peter R. March*

Above:
WR965 is now held in reserve, leaving No 8 Squadron with just five AEW aircraft. *both Peter R. March*

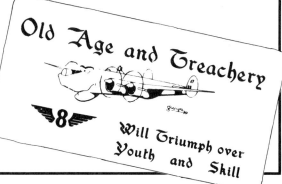

Old Age and Treachery

8

Will Triumph over Youth and Skill

Squadron's strength consisted of 12 operational aircraft. It also has to be remembered that the squadron is responsible for all its own training from conversion-to-type up to tactical exercises. Somehow it also finds time and aircraft to take part in air displays and to produce 'baddies' for RAF and NATO security exercises. On one occasion defence forces at an American base in England considered the best way of 'capturing' a Shackleton on the ground was to clamber aboard it in very large boots via the tailplane. In theory the 'enemy bomber' was captured, but the UK's AEW strength was seriously reduced until engineering officers from Lossiemouth were able to travel south and pronounce it safe to fly again.

In the 'direction' phase of the task, the Shackletons, like any other AEW aircraft, become airborne fighter control centres, vectoring UK Air Defence System interceptors such as Phantoms and Lightnings on to such real intruders as 'Bear' and 'Bisons' – happily so far just to photograph them, exchange waves and discourage them from venturing any further in a Westward direction. All the variations on these themes are of course continually practised under exercise conditions.

All three phrases of the AEW task are still carried out remarkably efficiently in the Shackletons by the latest version of the AN/APS radar which now has the symbols (F) I added to its designation meaning that it is the 'Mark Foxtrot Improved' version of the post-Pearl Harbor invention. In the AEW Shackletons the radar installation provides for three operator positions and consoles compared with two in the RN Gannets, and five operators are normally embarked, their leader, a commissioned officer, holding the title of 'TACO' (Tactical Co-ordinator). This allows for two of the radar operators (who apart from the TACO will either be junior commissoned officers, 'Master' warrant officers, Flight Sergeants or Sergeants) to be off-watch at a time during a typical eight or nine-hour sortie. Even though one of the off-watch crew will be cooking or serving meals and drinks and another manning radios and log-keeping, the system does mean that two out of the five will be relaxing from the special concentration required in operating an eyeball-and-chinagraph-pencil generation radar set. Operations and exercises over the North Sea demand especial concentration from the radar crewmen with the mass of oil rigs and shipping presenting a maze of 'paints' which have to be distinguished from those of fast-moving aircraft, the latter of which have to be classified into airliners and helicopters about their rightful business, until a potential 'real' or exercise target is identified.

Good as it still is, and even with such refinements as ground stabilisation from the aircraft's Doppler and North stabilisation always putting North at the top of the display, plus MTI (Moving Target Indicator) cutting out some of the returns from surface vessels, the dear old AN/APS 20 is a demanding piece of kit to work, particularly since its picture on a 7in scope, smaller than the average portable TV screen, is often

confused by 'sea returns' – white patches recording breaking waves. This last factor often determines the height at which a barrier patrol is flown; the rougher the sea the wider the area of 'sea return' showing itself directly below the aircraft. In essence the No 8 Squadron Shackletons are usually looking over the horizon to distances of up to about 150 miles beyond the radius at low level of the chain of ground radar stations extending down the east coast of Britain from Shetland southwards.

The other relevant equipment carried in the No 8 Squadron Shackletons includes the fairly venerable 'Orange Harvest' passive electronic countermeasures set which at least gives crews an indication that enemy radar signals are being aimed at them. The 'giant sparking plug' on the fuselage top is the outward and visible sign of 'Orange Harvest' in the AEW Mk 2s. The AEW Shackletons also carry APX 7 IFF (Identification Friend or Foe) interrogators and two V/UHF and two HF radio communication sets. In addition to the radar team of five the normal crew comprises the two pilots, an aircraft navigator and a flight engineer.

In its early days No 8 Squadron pilots were in the main former Shackleton maritime reconnaissance hands and throughout the past 14 years it has had the benefit of their experience, several returning to the type after tours on Nimrods. They have included several with more than 10,000 hours on the type with the names of the late Sqn Ldr Ian Weir and of Sqn Ldr (Retd) John Elias being especially revered – the latter notched up more than 13,000 hours on Shackletons and 17,000 overall.

Above:
WL756 with its undercarriage down. *Daniel J. March*

A number of pilots have, however, been converted within the Squadron's Training Flight from jets at a fairly early stage in their careers. An indication that the Shackletons would have to serve on for some time was given in 1984 when a new QFI (Qualified Flying Instructor) was appointed, as well as a new Commanding Officer, Wg Cdr Malcolm Cooper, who is a Navigator.

Training in the radar and AEW techniques was initially carried out by attached Fleet Air Arm Observer officers who had served in the Gannets – a happy arrangement because Lossiemouth was the shore 'home' of the last Naval Air Squadron to fly the type, No 849. Many of the RN officers stayed to stiffen the Shackleton crews during the early operational years.

A notable self-reliance feature of the training of the 'back-end' crews was the creation of Simulator/ Systems Trainer No 83987, otherwise known as 'The Dodo'. With the help of Marconi Elliott Avionics Systems Ltd and a modest amount of taxpayers' money the simulator was built on site from the fuselage of Shackleton MR2 WR967, within squadron resources, and handed over on 14 August 1975. It has worked hard ever since, making an important contribution to the conservation of airframe life among the flying aircraft. Its full mock-up of the rear end of the interior of an AEW Shackleton provides a flying environment for both newly joined crewmen and for those on continuation training.

A control room alongside houses 12 target generators for injection into the three standard radar displays. All the 'nasties' such as ECM noise jamming, sea returns and equipment faults can of course be fed in by the non-too-sadistic instructors who are all part of the squadron's normal flying complement.

On the engineering side the squadron remains unique in having its own built-in organisation instead of having to draw on the resources of a Station Engineering Wing. In consists of about 100 technicians commanded by a SENGO (Senior Engineering Officer) of Squadron Leader rank plus a small civilian team from British Aerospace Woodford. The squadron hangars at Lossiemouth constitute an aircraft factory in miniature, with a substantial stock in hand of complete Griffon power units including sets of the all-important contra-rotating propellor assemblies. Again the squadron 'converts' engine

technicians from jet to piston-prop skills and has no difficulty in obtaining the best of the breed, enormous interest and pride being taken in working with the superb Rolls-Royce machinery dating back to the 1950s in construction, and even further back in design. Privileged visitors to No 8 Squadron's hangars often note that their guides will be almost physically caressing the more intimate parts of a Griffon making (perhaps unfairly) such remarks as 'They don't make them like this any more'.

On results, I can only quote some records looked up for me which showed that for two months back, four out of the total strength of six aircraft had been 'on the line' by 09.00hrs most days, never less than three. On the bad days four were on the line by 12.00hrs.

During the continued period of uncertainty about the final handover of AEW responsibility to the Nimrod 3s, which continued until early 1985, one was assured that there were still plenty of airframe hours left in the last six Shackletons – they were all re-sparred during the 1970s conversion – to maintain at least a basic cover and a continuation of the state of the art among crews. Nevertheless the SENGO (Senior Engineering Officer) and others were having to be cautious about flying programmes, especially those involving roller landings which are an essential part of

8 SCREWS

ARE BETTER THAN TWO BLOW-JOBS

pilot continuation training as well as conversions. With the best of wills and skills these, nor the essential practice asymmetrics, do not always fall into the 'wouldn't have cracked an egg' category with a very heavy tail-wheeled aircraft which has historically been 'a bit of a handful', particularly in crosswinds.

With the forecast made in early 1985 of another two years operational life being required of the No 8 Squadron aircraft a joint RAF/British Aerospace examination programme was launched to check on fatigue life. The policy which led to the scrapping and burning of four of the AEW2 aircraft after the 'John Nott cut' seemed in hindsight to have been particularly

Left:
Sqn Ldr John Elias. *RAF Lossiemouth*

Below:
Shackletons make good settings for squadron photographs. Two members of No 8 Squadron (on wing to starboard side of fuselage) obviously could not quite keep their eyes on the birdie however when this picture was taken in 1981. *RAF Lossiemouth*

Above right:
The aircraft in this group picture of the ground crew of the JASS Flight at Ballykelly in 1955 is believed to be WR967, still serving faithfully as 'Dodo', the No 8 Squadron simulator. *W.L. White*

inept. Indeed there was a standing joke at Manchester Air and Space Museum where WR960 resides in apparently pristine condition that 'any day now the RAF will knock on the door and say "Please may we have our aeroplane back – we want to fly it again." '. A

considerable amount of fun and panache was exhibited by No 8 Squadron from the time of its re-formation, beginning with the painting of its fighter squadron yellow, blue and red flashes fore-and-aft of the fuselage roundels of the Shackletons, plus the Gambia Knife symbol inherited from periods of its history in and around Aden, the first in the 1920s with DH9As and Fairey IIIFs, another in the 1950s/1960s with Venoms and Hunters. By 1985, however, the joke of operating anachronisms was beginning to wear a little thin.

No 8 Squadron artists are noted for their sticker and T-Shirt designs, some of which are reproduced. For several years the No 8 Squadron aircraft were individually named after characters in the TV children's series 'Magic Roundabout' and 'The Herbs', the origin of this practice having something to do with the roundabout nature of AEW missions and also the behaviour of the T-4 VP293 on arrival, which bounced a bit and earned the name of 'Zebedee'. A latter day CO disapproved of the practice but for the record the original 12 AEW Mk 2s of No 8 Squadron were: WL745, 'Sage', WL756 'Mr Rusty', WL747 'Florence',

Above:
Mk 2 AEW Shackleton photographed from the Memorial Flight Lancaster. This is a 'still' from the film *End of an Era* made for television in 1984. *Stanley Hitchcock*

Right:
Boo-boo and Octavia.

WR960 'Dougal', WR963 'Parsley', WL757 'Brian', WL790 'Mr MacHenry', WL795 'Rosalie', WL741 'PC Knapweed', WL793 'Ermintrude' WR965 'Dill' and WL754 'Paul'. The last six remaining in service are WL756, WL747, WL963, WL757, WL790 and WR965.

Towards the end of 1984 one of these aircraft was held back in reserve, to cater for the possibility of some major overhauls having to be conducted at British Aerospace, Woodford, in order to keep the AEW presence going until the Nimrod 3 could finally take its place in front-line service. At time of writing the reserve aircraft was WR965, earlier known as 'Dill'. In early 1985 therefore, when the further delay in the Nimrod AEW 3 had been clarified, No 8 Squadron and the nation at large had only *five* aircraft providing airborne early warning cover as its contribution to NATO defences in this important field. Many explanations were offered and proffered in Parliament and in the press, and especially on a 'Panorama' programme, for the continuing delay over the Nimrod 3. In spite of all these it came down to No 8 Squadron and its last remaining Shackletons to fill the gap for

whatever had gone wrong in the high technology world.

The Squadron also acts as parent unit to two remarkable winged members of the Royal Air Force's numerical strength, the eagle owls Boo-boo and Octavia. Boo-boo originally entered RAF service as a bird-strike counter-measure but was suspected of suffering from vertigo as his maximum preferred altitude seemed to be about 6ft. Octavia was found for him as a mate and so named by young BBC 'Blue Peter' viewers in 1980. The pair live quietly and in harmony just outside squadron HQ and pleased all concerned by raising young during 1983 and 1984.

8
The last of the many

Although much sadness has been expressed over the number of Shackletons reduced to scrap or ending their days ignominiously as training aids for fire crews, up until 1984 four non-flying examples were maintained in museums in Britain and two stood as gate guardians at RAF stations. Several others seemed destined to remain on permanent exhibition in South Africa.

Mr Peter Thomas of Lairg, Sutherland, the aviation historian and enthusiast who was largely instrumental in obtaining one of the last Sunderlands for the Hendon RAF Museum, was active in 1984 in a campaign to preserve one of the last No 8 Squadron aircraft in flying condition, possibly as an addition to the RAF Memorial Flight. His project, which was attracting many thousands of signatures, was thought to have the chance of a 'following wind' since the No 8

Squadron Shackletons have been used to provide continuous training and check-outs for the crews of the Memorial Flight Lancaster *City of Lincoln*.

The preserved aircraft in the UK at the time of writing were:

T-4 VP293 ('Zebedee') at the Strathallan Air Museum. This historic aircraft began its career as one of the first Mk 1s delivered to No 236 OCU in 1951, served in No 224 Squadron at Gibraltar and with Nos 42 and 206 Squadrons at St Eval. It was converted into a T-4 trainer and served in this form with the Maritime Operational Unit. It later worked at Farnborough with

Below:
A symbolic picture taken during the making of Stanley Hitchcock's film *End of an Era*. Stanley Hitchcock

the Weapons Flight and one version of its 'Magic Roundabout' nickname is that it acquired it there – see the previous chapter for an alterative version! The aircraft was acquired by the Strathallan collection organisers in 1976 with the intention that it should be kept flying, but this clearly became beyond the resources available.

Mk 2 (MR) WL795: gate guardian at RAF St Mawgan.

Mk 2 (MR) WL738: gate guardian at RAF Lossiemouth (with dummy AEW radome added).

Above left:
Another shot taken at Lossiemouth during the making of *End of an Era*. Unfortunately several of the Mk 2 AEW aircraft grounded druing the 'Nott Cut' of 1981 ended up in this state, although an attempt was made to keep one as a public exhibit at RAF Valley. *Stanley Hitchcock*

Left and above:
'Zebedee' (VP293) at Strathallan in 1980. *Dr Alan Curry*

Below:
The last Mk 3 Phase 3 to fly arriving at Duxford on 22 August 1972.

Mk 3 (Phase 3) XF708 at Imperial War museum airfield, Duxford.

Mk 3 WR977 at Newark Air Museum.

Mk 2 AEW WR960 at Manchester Air and Space Museum.

Until 1984 No 8 Squadron engineers were still cannibalising internal parts, particularly wiring harnesses, from the Lossiemouth gate guard WL738. Meanwhile enthusiastic volunteers in Manchester were restoring the interior of WR960 with the intention of making it a 'walk through' exhibit.

Four Mk3s and one Mk 2 were still in a reasonable

Above:
The one which did *not* get burnt. Mk 2 AEW WR960 arriving at Cosford to be sectionalised before re-assembly inside the Manchester Air and Space Museum. *City of Manchester Public Relations*

Below:
Re-assembling WR960. *Dr Alan Curry*

Right:
WR960 shortly before the opening of the Manchester Air and Space Museum in 1983. *Dr Alan Curry*

Below right:
Lovingly polished. *Dr Alan Curry*

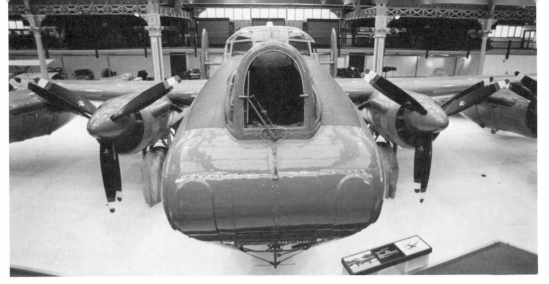

state of preservation at No 2 School of Technical Training, RAF Cosford, used for instruction on hydraulic systems, etc. Mk 2 WL801, which had erroneously been described as being on public show at the Cosford RAF Museum, was reduced to scrap in October 1984.

Apart from Mr Thomas's project many other groups were bent on preserving the last of the Shackletons, including an association of former 'Ballykelly hands' in Northern Ireland, and some senior executives of British Aerospace (formerly Avro) at Woodford. Certainly 'the Lovely Old Beast' was not going to be allowed just to fade away.

Above:
Dominating the scene.   *Dr Alan Curry*

Below:
WL798 at No 2 School of Technical Training, RAF Cosford.   *Dr Alan Curry*